Mae West

She Who Laughs, Lasts

American Biographical History Series

Mae West
She Who Laughs, Lasts

June Sochen
Northeastern Illinois University

Harlan Davidson, Inc.
Arlington Heights, Illinois 60004

Library of Congress Cataloging-in-Publication Data

Sochen, June, 1937–
    Mae West : She who laughs, lasts / June Sochen.
    p. cm.—(The American biographical history series)
Includes bibliographical references and index.
ISBN 0-88295-891-7
1. West, Mae. 2. Motion picture actors and actresses—United
States—Biography. I. Title. II. Series.
PN2287.W4566S65 1992
791.43'028'092—DC20
[B]   91-42533
                                                 CIP

Book design: Roger Eggers
Cover and frontispiece photographs provided by
Picture This (Philadelphia)

Manufactured in the United States of America
96   95   94   93   92   1   2   3   4   5   MG

EDITORS' FOREWORD

As biographies offer access to the past, they reflect the needs of the present. Newcomers to biography and biographical history often puzzle over the plethora of books that some lives inspire. "Why do we need so many biographies of Abraham Lincoln?" they ask, as they search for the "correct" version of the sixteenth president's story. Each generation needs to revisit Lincoln because each generation has fresh questions, inspired by its own experiences. Collectively, the answers to these questions expand our understanding of Lincoln and America in the 1860s, but they also assist us to better comprehend our own time. People concerned with preserving such civil liberties as freedom of the press in time of national crisis have looked at Lincoln's approach to political opposition during and after secession. Civil rights activists concerned with racial injustice have turned to Lincoln's life to clarify unresolved social conflicts that persist more than a century after his assassination.

Useful as it is to revisit such lives, it is equally valuable to explore those often neglected by biographers. Almost always, biographies are written about prominent individuals who changed, in some measure, the world around them. But who is prominent and what constitutes noteworthy change are matters of debate. Historical beauty is definitely in the eye of the beholder. That most American biographies tell of great white males and their untainted accomplishments speaks volumes about the society that produced such uncritical paeans. More recently, women and men of various racial, religious, and economic backgrounds have expanded the range of American biography. The lives of prominent African-American leaders, Native American chief-

tains, and immigrant sweatshop workers who climbed the success ladder to its top now crowd onto those library shelves next
to familiar figures.

In the American Biographical History Series, specialists in
key areas of American history describe the lives of important
men and women of many different races, religions, and ethnic
backgrounds as those figures shaped and were shaped by the political, social, economic, and cultural issues of their day and the
people with whom they lived. Biographical subjects and readers
share a dialogue across time and space as biographers pose the
questions suggested by life in modern-day America to those who
lived in other eras. Each life offers a timeless reservoir of answers
to questions from the present. The result is at once edifying and
entertaining.

The concise biographical portrait found in each volume in
this series is enriched and made especially instructive by the attention paid to generational context. Each biographer has taken
pains to link his or her subject to peers and predecessors engaged in the same area of accomplishment. Even the rare individuals whose ideas or behavior transcend their age operated
within a broad social context of values, attitudes, and beliefs.
Iconoclastic radicals, too, whatever their era, owed a debt to earlier generations of protesters and left a legacy for those who
would resist the status quo in the future.

Biographers in the series offer readers new companions, individuals of accomplishment, whose lives and works can be
weighed and assessed and consulted as resources in answering
the nagging questions that the thoughtful in every generation
ask of the past to better comprehend the present. The makers of
America—male and female, black and white and red and yel-
low, Christian, Moslem, Jew, atheist, agnostic, and polytheist,
rich and poor and in between—all testify with their lives that the
past is prologue. Anxious to share his rich experiences with
those willing to listen, an elderly Eastern European immigrant
living in Pittsburgh boasted, "By myself, I'm a book!" He, too,

realized that an important past could be explicated through the narrative of a life, in fact, his own.

When a biographer sees his or her subject in broader context, important themes are crystallized, an era is illuminated. The single life becomes a window to a past age and its truths for succeeding generations and for you.

ALAN M. KRAUT
JON L. WAKELYN

CONTENTS

Editors' Foreword   v

Preface   xi

ONE

"I'd Rather Be Looked Over than
Overlooked," 1893–1922   1

TWO

"She Went Up the Ladder of Success, Wrong by
Wrong," 1923–1932   32

THREE

"Goodness Had Nothing to Do with It," 1933–1943   57

FOUR

"I Like Two Kinds of Men: Foreign and
Domestic," 1944–1964   96

FIVE

"Be Cool and Collect," 1965–1980 and Beyond   120

Bibliographical Essay   142

Index   146

PREFACE

From the general to the particular: I have been researching, lecturing, and writing about American women for over twenty years and have written surveys on the subject as well as specialized studies. However, this is my first effort at biography. Looking at Mae West's life was an interesting opportunity to examine the unique and representative features of women's experience. To study a popular cultural figure whose identity was tied to sensational themes added spice to the endeavor.

As in every project, there are a number of debts to acknowledge. The librarians at the New York Public Library's Theater Collection were particularly helpful. My colleague Fred MacDonald, whose private collection of popular culture material is incredible, gave me some rare Mae West playbills as well as hard-to-find movie magazine articles. His constant enthusiasm and cooperation on this book are very much appreciated. My editor, Alan Kraut, was encouraging, efficient, and helpful. The editor-in-chief at Harlan Davidson, Maureen Gilgore Hewitt, was also very supportive and committed to this project. I would also like to thank the anonymous reviewer for her/his very useful comments.

Comedian Kate Clinton originated the witticism that is the title of this book: she who laughs, lasts—good advice to all people in every time period and advice by which Mae West lived.

JUNE SOCHEN

Mae West in costume as Diamond Lil. Photograph provided by Picture This (Philadelphia).

CHAPTER ONE

I'd Rather Be Looked Over than Overlooked

1893–1922

A biography of Mae West that places her among the prominent entertainers and commentators on American culture is long overdue. Celebrity pieces, interviews, and fans' recollections of her abound. However, the student of American history and culture looks in vain for a study that takes seriously the comic bawdiness of Mae West. To people under the age of forty, Mae West is probably a shadowy historical character. But to those who have seen her in person, or one of her movies, or her rare television appearances in the 1960s, her name brings a smile. Also, to collectors of nostalgic posters and postcards, Mae West still exists. Those who recall her remember that she was identified with sexuality and sex, but to today's teenagers, she must appear tame—fully clothed, somewhat overweight by today's fashion, perhaps a mature version of Madonna. The legendary status she attained during her life may be completely unknown to current followers of popular culture.

During her long life, Mae West evoked strong responses. Often, smiles and laughter; but from the humorless, stern frowns and pinched lips. West learned early in her show business career that humor was a valuable weapon in the battle between the sexes and in the struggle to gain a following. In a period when women's roles on the theatrical stage were clearly defined (with comic not being one of them), Mae West winked, smirked, laughed, and joked about sex, the forbidden subject. As a result, she became the symbol of the daring, sexy woman who made fun of sex. In prudish America, she kidded her audience, the censors, and all others who believed in the double sexual standard, in woman's passivity, and in their own moral seriousness. West emphasized her sexual allure, assuring everyone that she knew how desirable she was. Was she a self-parodist or was she seriously touting her female assets? Audiences were not always sure, which contributed to her appeal. She boldly asserted her worth, her uniqueness, and her specialness in an age when women were trained to be modest, not boastful.

She exposed hypocrisy and male arrogance, all with a smile. In a public space, often before a largely male audience, she crossed the boundary between polite and rude—and got applause and large salaries for doing it. Mae West's risqué act attracted rowdy college men as well as working-class, middle- and upper-class men. Women rarely attended as they knew in advance that a West show was directed to the male gender. But many women attended her later Broadway shows and, still later, her movies. One of the unusual features of her career was that she broadened her audience as she went from medium to medium; she gained women followers from her movies and, in the 1950s, from her night club act.

Mae West deserves a modern biography because she provides a window on the world of early twentieth-century entertainment, an interesting perspective on women entertainers (a group usually neglected in studies of American women), and insights into the varying tastes of the American public. Entertainers often walk the thin line between unconventionality and conventionality. They test society's limits as well as confirm them. Mae West challenged the boundaries more than any other entertainer, and although she paid some penalties for her outrageousness, she also enjoyed celebrity status and the adoration of her fans.

The longevity of Mae West's career gave her an advantage over most entertainers of her time. Few made successful transitions from vaudeville to the Broadway stage, to the movies, and then to night clubs. Few entertainers enjoyed a fifty-year career. Few lived long enough to preserve and protect their images and reputations. Few entertainers, male or female, planned and controlled their careers as completely as did Mae West. Her name appeared on most of her movie scripts, either as screenwriter or as contributor of original dialogue. For all of these reasons, Mae West's life and career lends new understanding to our knowledge of twentieth-century show business, women's history, and American cultural history.

That popular culture figures deserve inclusion in discussions of America's cultural history is just beginning to be understood. Although scholars and intellectuals receive ample attention in history textbooks, monographs, and courses, little notice is given to the popular heroes and heroines of our past. Baseball stars such as Babe Ruth may be included, because America's favorite pastime is given token mention; some movie stars also may be discussed briefly, because movies were a major industry as well as a leisure-time activity during the Depression. But entertainers who began their careers in vaudeville or on the Broadway stage are rarely included in discussions of American culture in the early twentieth century, the period in which Mae West began her career.

As Lawrence Levine has noted in *High Brow/Low Brow,* by the late nineteenth century the economic classes had separated in their popular commercial amusements. Although the working, middle, and upper classes had mingled, albeit uneasily, in the same theaters earlier in the century, divergent tastes, finances, and values caused new forms of entertainments to arise and new forms of segregation to be imposed. Opera became the elite's bailiwick, whereas burlesque attracted the working classes. Art museums and symphony orchestra halls raised their prices and standards of decorum, thereby discouraging attendance by working-class people. In the burlesque and vaudeville houses, by contrast, the less affluent were welcomed. Early burlesque houses served up liquor as well as provided variety acts. Chorus girls, jugglers, animal acts, comics, and Shakespearean actors all worked in burlesque. Simultaneously, the vaudeville house emerged as a more respectable venue for much of the same kinds of entertainment. Entrepreneur Tony Pastor has been credited with bringing respectability to the variety show in the 1890s and catering to family audiences. But at the turn of the century, many performers moved from burlesque to vaudeville with ease and the two houses appeared more alike than different. As competition increased between them, as well as from other forms of entertainment, burlesque became broader, cruder, and more vulgar, and vaudeville eventually disappeared, losing out to the movie palace.

The lower rungs of the entertainment ladder have not yet achieved sufficient respectability for scholars to take them seriously. Yet it was in vaudeville, burlesque, and night clubs that Americans first witnessed public audacity as well as ethnic variety. Burlesque and night clubs, the former appealing mostly to working-class and college men and the latter attracting middle- and upper-class couples, provided audiences with bawdy women singers, black and white, immigrant and native. It was in the shady night spots that black audiences heard Bessie Smith sing suggestive lyrics as she wiggled around the stage; in burlesque, the women singers made explicit what had to be implied in the more respectable setting of vaudeville. Upper-class men looked at nearly nude women in these public environments while middle- and working-class men enjoyed the same experiences. All classes and both genders' views of flamboyance, of excitement, and adventure were acquired in these places. Surely their view that women were either virgins or whores (with the entertainers in the latter category) were confirmed here. Women entertainers at the bawdy end of the spectrum, such as Mae West, expressed the image of woman as sensual temptress, but combined it with a newer, more audacious one—the independent woman. West, Smith, and their colleagues showed spunk, spirit, and individualism in their performances, thereby giving audiences an additional image of women to consider.

Respectable women of both races and all classes did not frequent the burlesque houses; some attended vaudeville shows, although they sometimes turned their backs when a bawdy woman entertainer appeared. Burlesque queen Millie De Leon, for example, tried to taunt women who would not watch her outrageous act. But women heard about the shows and they often saw the women performers' pictures in the newspapers. They may not have had the direct experience of their husbands, fathers, brothers, and sons, but they surely heard secondhand reports or whispered references about the performers.

The image of woman as Eve has been dominant in popular culture for a long time. Images of woman as sexual temptress, as bold initiator of sexual activity, and as outside the realm of respectability have existed in novels, plays, and music for hundreds of years and, in this century, radio, movies and television. James Fenimore Cooper's novels always featured a fair-haired "good" woman and a raven-haired temptress. In the twentieth century, Mae West, Jean Harlow, and a host of other blondes played Eves. They defied the stereotype by looking virginal and behaving like whores. The further twist that Mae West added to this longstanding image was that she succeeded—she remained dominant and central at the end of the play or movie, in sharp contrast to most whores, good-hearted, blonde, or otherwise, who lost the man and often their lives at the end of the story.

Mae West competed with many Eves in the early twentieth-century, but finally distinguished herself from the multitude in New York and became a star on the vaudeville and Broadway stages. Later, with the help of a formidable Hollywood movie studio during the 1930s, she became a superstar. Still later, through constant self-promotion and continuous activity, she became a celebrity like Elizabeth Taylor in the 1990s, a famous person whose name and figure were immediately recognizable to large numbers of people even after her active career had ended. Mae West achieved enduring fame by developing a distinctive persona and promoting it so assiduously that its potentially offensive features became part of its strength and resilience. As a celebrity for over thirty years, she enjoyed regular media coverage; she had only to appear at a premiere or a party to ensure that her picture would be in the next day's newspaper.

Star, superstar, celebrity. These are three levels of success to which entertainers aspire.* Any one of them is desirable and enviable, though the few that achieve celebrity status are viewed as rare and very special. Mae West has the distinction of being one of the few performers from the early years of the twentieth century who became all three.

Mae West's longevity as a performer and celebrity enabled her to entertain at least three generations of Americans. She took to the stage at the age of seven and remained an active performer until she was close to seventy years old. Indeed, she continued to make public appearances into her eighties. Most entertainers eventually either burn out or find themselves without an audience. West spent the years from 1907 to 1928 creating and perfecting a persona that would assure her of continued box-office success: the 1890s good-time gal, Diamond Lil. During the process, she played to packed houses. As she shaped her characteristic gestures, audiences laughed, shouted, and demanded more. Even as she aged and her self-parody became more exaggerated, the crowds kept coming. By the late 1940s, when she was close to fifty years old, she had become an institution. Young people went to the theater to see the latest revival of *Diamond Lil* so they could say that yes, they had actually seen the *real* Mae West. Her night club acts of the 1950s, her film appearance in the 1970 debacle, *Myra Breckinridge,* her interviews in American magazines and newspapers during the 1960s and 1970s, and the reruns of her old movies kept her in the public eye long after her contemporaries had retired and died.

---

*In the lexicon used here, a star's fame rests upon the success of his or her latest picture or play; a superstar has audiences lined up for every movie and performance, and a celebrity has enduring fame and attention beyond the active years of performance.

Although the biographical details of her early years are somewhat sketchy, some things are known for sure. Mary Jane West was born on August 17, 1893, on Bushwick Avenue in Brooklyn, New York. Her father was John Patrick West, of English-Irish descent, and her mother was Matilda Doelger West, an immigrant from Bavaria, Germany. Other things are less certain. Mae West gave a number of different accounts of her father's occupation. Sometimes she said he was a prize fighter; at other times she said he was an owner of a livery stable (which he was); and at still other times, she claimed he was a doctor or a detective. We do know that Mary Jane became May when she entered amateur talent shows at the age of seven. She later changed the spelling to Mae because, as she explained in her autobiography, the "e" was up and the "y" was down. This whimsicality would be exhibited in a hundred ways after she achieved fame. When reporters, by whom she was constantly hounded after she became a star, asked her about her background, her answer depended upon her mood. She even claimed to be of different religions on different occasions.

It also is certain that Mae West was the oldest in a family of three children. She had a sister named Beverly, who was born five years after her, and a brother, John, born a year after Beverly. By most accounts, Mae West grew up in comfortable middle-class surroundings, in a three-story brownstone in Brooklyn on a tree-lined street of one-family homes. Her desire to perform appeared early. In her autobiography, West commented that she was never jealous of her younger siblings because she was already preoccupied with herself. She began dancing lessons at the age of seven and appeared at an amateur night at the Royal Theater on Fulton Street in Brooklyn that same year, 1900. By her account, she won most every amateur talent show she entered.

As she later recalled, when the professional part of the evening's entertainment ended, the theater manager would step out to announce the amateurs. "Tell 'em they're welcome by a nice big hand, and show yer generosity by yer offerings tossed at them." Mae always received generous offerings. She was a small and delicate child, and she often wore her mother's big hat on stage in order to increase her height. With one hand holding her hat and the other on her hip, she developed a gesture at age seven that would become one of her adult trademarks. Her first song on stage was "Movin' Day," followed by a comedy dialect number called "My Mariooch-Make-Da-Hoochy-Ma-Coocha in Coney Island." Her versatility and her humor were already apparent.

Mae West's timing could not have been better. Her very young career began with the new century just as commercial entertainment was taking off in the growing cities of America. The new immigrants who congregated in New York City, for example, loved the new vaudeville houses. Although many ethnic groups continued to create their own entertainments in their own communities, many flocked to distinctly American forms of amusement; as part of their eagerness to assimilate, they participated in American popular culture. Immigrants also enjoyed the two-reeler silent films, which did not require that they understand English, and they attended the burlesque and vaudeville shows. The nickelodeons that showed the silent films seated between three hundred and five hundred people; from 1904 to 1914 they usually were filled all day for the continuous showings of the short films. On Saturday night, workers splurged on a vaudeville show. The peoples' enthusiasm for paid amusements seemed endless.

In 1896, for example, there were ten variety or vaudeville theaters in New York and six in Chicago. By 1910, New York had thirty-one such places and Chicago had twenty-two. By 1913, the number of vaudeville theaters in the United States had skyrocketed to 2,973; Brooklyn, New York, alone had fifty-three. Mae West once said that it would have taken her six years to play each vaudeville theater in the country one time. Enterprising businessmen quickly recognized the profit to be made in entertainment. They capitalized on the insatiable appetite of their customers, booking between ten and twenty acts into a vaude-

ville show, twice a day, seven days a week. Competitors tried to
outdo each other by offering bigger and better shows. Florenz
Ziegfeld, a Broadway producer, promised audiences spectacular
scenery, dazzling chorus lines, numerous costume changes,
singers, dancers, comics, and jugglers. His yearly Follies became a special treat for more affluent audiences.

Businessmen, many of whom had the same ethnic background as their customers, became theater owners, producers of
variety shows, and makers of the new silent film. Agent, director, writer, and designer were new occupations in the profit-
making show business industry. By the 1920s, show business was
exceeded in size only by the automobile industry. The most adventurous invested in show business, and the most visionary
planned to create networks of theaters across the country in
which to place their performers. Just as business magnates
strove to monopolize, so too did show business entrepreneurs.
The Loews, Keith and Albee, and the Shuberts brought to show
business the same management principles and capitalistic goals
that their contemporaries used in other industries. Indeed, show
business could be studied as easily as the steel or railroad business
to gain insights into the workings of capitalism in this century.

Amusements, previously self-developed and -defined, now
became highly structured activities; one had to plan attendance
at a prescribed time at a special place. Both the theater of
Broadway (New York City's main theater street) and the vaudeville house had specific show times, as well as a differentiated
price structure, depending upon where one sat in the theater.
The whole experience of attending an entertainment became
more formal and the choices multiplied; any night of the week,
a seeker of amusement had many options. As the audiences increased, so did the number of entertainers, the competition,
and the profits.

The variety of acts seen on America's stages reflected the incredible diversity of America's people. German comics spoke
with a German accent, white men sang in blackface, ethnic
comics exposed the frailties of their particular cultural group,

would-be actors rewrote Shakespeare to create a more updated version of King Lear's and Hamlet's tragedies, and everyone spoofed opera singers and politicians. Bawdy women singers made fun of Wagnerian sopranos and Strauss's favorite heroine, Salomé. Every self-respecting woman star of the period did Salomé's dance of the seven veils. Entertainers who started out in ethnic theaters strove to break out and appeal successfully to all Americans in vaudeville houses or on Broadway.

All Americans, native and immigrant alike, seemed to enjoy the novelty and diversity of the vaudeville house. A juggling act might be followed by an Italian singer, who might be followed by a cowboy-and-Indian act, and so on. There usually were nine acts before the intermission, which was followed by nine or ten additional acts. Audiences received a lot of entertainment for the price of admission. The headliner usually appeared twice during the evening, first as the eighth act before the intermission, and then in the middle of the second half of the show. A printed program indicated the order and nature of the acts.

This is the world Mae West entered when, at eight years old, she joined Hal Clarendon's Stock Company, located in Brooklyn at the Gotham Theater. She attended school irregularly and performed juvenile parts at the theater. Compulsory school attendance laws were not strictly enforced at the time; indeed, the overcrowded classrooms discouraged attendance, and the teachers preferred to have fewer children in class. There also were no strict laws regulating child labor. Although West's family did not rely on her earnings for their sustenance (in dramatic contrast to the families of most child entertainers), they did not object to her theatrical career.

Indeed, needy or approving parents were essential for child performers. In many show business biographies, child stars discussed how their earnings sustained the family. Mary Pickford, Eva Tanguay, Fanny Brice and countless others supported, or at least contributed, to their family's earnings. Amateur nights, where Mae West began, were normal venues for children. On a good night, they could earn fifty dollars, a much larger sum than their fathers could earn in a week of manual work. Black women entertainers such as Moms Mabley and Bessie Smith earned sums of money that were unimagined in their poor, rural southern households.

Whereas Tanguay's and Brice's earnings helped their families survive, West's parents encouraged her performing because she was irrepressible; she could not be stopped. Even as an eight-year-old, she was strong-willed and usually got her way. She quoted her father as saying of her at the time: "If they could bottle nerve, she'd have more than Rockefeller has oil." Sister Beverly later recalled: "She never did care to play with other children; they seemed silly to her." West herself acknowledged that she never had girl friends growing up; she was too busy preening and performing. She always seemed to have the upper hand with her parents. When she became successful, she in turn showered them with gifts and, somewhat reluctantly, lent a helping hand to her brother and sister.

The popular theater had many parts available for juvenile actors. Mae West began conventionally enough by playing the title role in *Little Nell the Marchioness,* a popular melodrama that had been around a long time. The play, an adaptation of Charles Dicken's *The Old Curiosity Shop,* had earlier established the reputation of Lotta Crabtree, a famous American comedienne-actress of the late nineteenth century. For six years, from the ages of eight to fourteen, Mae West played in various ingenue roles, usually in one of the many vaudeville houses or theaters in Brooklyn. Without going too far from home, she was able to gain substantial experience as a performer. She enjoyed applause, and each success convinced her even more that she had found her life's work. The stage had become her laboratory for learning. One of the things she had to learn was how to be a successful female in the difficult world of male-dominated entertainment.

As America entered the twentieth century, the rules of the Victorian age still applied. Respectable women were supposed to be passive, obedient first to their fathers and then to their hus-

bands, submissive in the home, demure in public, and respectful of male authority everywhere. Women dressed modestly,
never exposing their limbs or their bosoms. They lowered their
eyes when speaking; at appropriate times, they blushed. They
never spoke loudly or crudely; they rarely laughed aloud.
Women entertainers were thought to be outside this system. As
the evangelist Billy Sunday warned: "Young women should
shun the stage as they would the bubonic plague; the conditions
behind the footlights, especially for chorus girls and show girls,
is something horrible."

Some adventurous young women who were daring and curious ignored Billy Sunday's warnings. Even if the opportunities
in that new field were not limitless, even if they could not be the
star in the adventure, or the comic who delivered the punch line,
the show business allure was great. However small the roles and
opportunities were in vaudeville, many independent-minded
women found them better than the alternatives. Yet even in this
new forum, cultural rules about women's behavior still existed.
Women occupied clearly defined territory in show business.
They were the innocent victims in the melodramas and adventures, the sweet, young straight person in the comic duo, the
pretty singer, or the dancer in the chorus line. Few women comics were featured in burlesque, vaudeville, or Broadway shows.
After all, comedy was physical and vulgar. It meant slipping on
a banana peel or having a pie thrown in your face, unbecoming
and unladylike behavior. The witty dialogue, the effective
punch lines, were always delivered by the man; the pretty young
woman (and she was always young) stood there, looking prop-
erly demure.

The conventions of fiction and entertainment reflected the
Victorian code regarding gender roles and behaviors. The stage
was as male-dominated as the office, the government, and the
home. American culture's unspoken rules about woman's
proper place applied to the theater. Most women in show business accepted their restricted place, glad to have a role at all in
this exciting new medium. After all, the wages were still better

for most of them than they would be in alternative employments as domestics, factory workers, or salesclerks in the new retail stores. There was glamour and the possibility of fame and fortune in show business. The other choices held no such promise. The qualifications for show business jobs were rather clearly defined: a good figure; rudimentary dancing ability for the chorus line; singing talent for a featured role; and just a pretty face seemed all that was necessary for the male comic's straight woman.

Of course, real talent was always an important asset for both male and female entertainers. When Fanny Brice first appeared in the Ziegfeld Follies in 1910, everyone knew she was a winner. When Al Jolson sang on the same stage, his ability was also immediately noticed. But for many performers, the pathway to recognition and success was slower, made up of small victories until the big chance or the big billing ensured stardom. Then the challenge was maintaining the star position. For most, of course, stardom never came. The majority of entertainers contented themselves with small roles in other peoples' successes. The competition for even the smallest role was ferocious. And staying in the running was expensive. Actors paid, out of their meager earnings, for new songs and new skits; they also rented halls for their rehearsals at their own expense.

The acts in vaudeville shows had to be changed regularly. The audience's taste for novelty, freshness, and variety seemed insatiable. Entertainers had to pay for new material, new routines, new songs and new costumes. The schedule of this demanding occupation required a vaudevillian to travel from town to town doing two shows a day, six days a week. The vaudeville circuit included small towns, mid-size cities, and the "big time"—large vaudeville houses in Manhattan, Brooklyn, the Bronx, Chicago, and Philadelphia. Some places had a seating capacity of 1,500 to 2,000 people. Some circuits toured New England; others traveled to the Midwest.

There was a separate vaudeville circuit for black entertainers, the Theatrical Owners Booking Association, known among black vaudevillians as "Tough on Black Asses." The accommodations, the theaters, and the traveling arrangements were inferior to those available for white vaudevillians. But the profession was growing for talented and ambitious people of both races. The National Vaudeville Artists Association was formed in 1916, and within a year it had 6,000 active members. An advocate claimed: "Vaudeville is the best paid profession in the world. More two-a-day artists own their own homes than in any other branch of the theatre."

Each night the vaudeville houses were filled. Customarily, Friday night was family night, whereas Wednesday night was often a fund raiser for some worthy cause. The upper classes had their night, as did the working class. Mae West once recalled that the theater manager helped performers by telling them who was in the audience each night. West claimed that she changed her act more often than most, although it was considered bad luck to change a successful routine, because she got bored quickly. She was amazed at the quantity of vaudeville houses in large and small communities around the country.

All vaudevillians were reminded that the customers had to be respected: no foul language on stage and no lewd gestures. In the Keith-Albee houses, a backstage sign reminded the entertainers that neither the word "slob" nor the expression "son of a gun" could be used. Imagine the agony of the theater manager who tried to control Mae West's act. It was hard, however, to censor her performance, as the actual lyrics of her songs contained no risqué words; it was how she said something, as the critics wryly noted, rather than what she said that was objectionable to the moralists. Dancers, also, were hard to restrain and control. Audiences loved the bawdy performers, and the managers were torn between the scrutiny of the censors and the happy applause of the crowd. They usually sided with the audience.

At fourteen, in 1907, Mae West joined the national vaudeville circuit. Through the United Booking Office, the booking arm of the Keith-Albee vaudeville circuit, she was engaged by vaudeville houses all over America. When Mae West signed up with the UBO, she was on the ground floor of a theatrical operation that was to monopolize vaudeville. Keith-Albee owned many theaters, and in cities where they did not own a vaudeville house, they acted as the middlemen, booking the acts for the local theater owners. Just as the steel, oil, and railroad businesses were beginning to display monopolistic tendencies, so too was the vaudeville business.

Although West interrupted her vaudeville career with appearances on Broadway in musical reviews, she was primarily a vaudevillian from her debut in 1907 until 1918. She clearly displayed spunk and talent early on; the variety show's many singers, dancers, jugglers, and comics all vied for the audience's favor, and newcomers could have a difficult time. A poorly received act literally got the hook—a man in the wings used the crook of a cane to yank the unsuccessful performer off the stage. The competition for bookings, therefore, was keen. According to one account, there were over 20,000 vaudevillians seeking about 8,000 positions by 1915. Mae West quickly learned the rules of the theater and changed her material to suit the audience.

She toured with Willie Hogan in a Huck Finn act in which she played the Sis Hopkins role, a sweet young country girl in a sunbonnet, gingham dress, and lace-trimmed bloomers. Sis Hopkins was the standard first acting role for most young women. The able and enterprising went on to more challenging fare. Mae West was already showing her ambitious nature and dogged determination to succeed. While on tour, she met a performer named Frank Wallace. Around 1910, they teamed up and created a song-and-dance routine. A personal as well as a professional relationship ensued. In Milwaukee, on April 11, 1911, the seventeen-year-old West married Wallace. This was to be her only marriage in a long life in which romance played an active and continuous role.

The marriage ended almost as soon as it began. According to West, young as she was, she recognized that it was a mistake.

She later wrote in her autobiography, "This one weird experience with matrimony made me respect the institution." Although Wallace would reappear in her life later, seeking alimony and making life difficult for her, they parted during the first year of the marriage and West did not bother until many years later to divorce him. In 1911, although still a teenager, her life experience was dramatically different from that of her cohorts. Most seventeen-year-old women were unmarried, either working if they were from poor families, or in school if they were part of the growing middle class. She found soul mates, however, and similar experiences among her show business sisters. Sophie Tucker, for example, had married at sixteen and separated a year later. Brief marriages, as well as frequent and temporary relationships with men, characterized the lives of many women entertainers.

Given their lifestyles, it was difficult for women entertainers to maintain a stable romantic tie. If the women were successful, as Tucker and West were, it was even harder to preserve fragile male egos. The men in their lives quickly tired of being known only as the paramours of famous women. Although most American women gladly took on their husbands' name and identity, American men were not so inclined. To be known as, for example, Mr. Mae West was a sex-role reversal not uncommon among show business couples but still an atypical and undesirable arrangement for most men. According to dominant cultural values and roles, men were the breadwinners, and women stayed at home. Mae West and her sisters in entertainment upset society's standards here as well as on the stage. As working women who earned more than most men, they were rarities; as famous women, they defied the dominant image of women as demure and modest. Neither Mae West nor her colleagues articulated conscious challenges to conventional mores on gender roles, but they lived them.

Eva Tanguay, Mae West's most compelling rival in the 1910s and early 1920s, was the biggest star in vaudeville, commanding a weekly salary of $3,500. West was earning around $500 a week

then, no mean amount at a time when working men were re-
ceiving about $2 for a ten-hour day. West admired Tanguay and
was quoted as saying of her: "There are two kinds of headliners
in vaudeville—the kind that draws and the kind that makes
good, with occasionally a combination of the two, like Eva Tanguay, who does both." Mae West watched and listened to the
public reactions to Tanguay. She paid attention to the details of
her performance that made the audiences scream. Tanguay's
show was described by one commentator as "assault and bat-
tery." Tanguay sang: "When I put on tights/My name went up
in lights." West also studied Tanguay's skill at self-promotion
and her self-parody based on a wildly anarchic sense of humor.

West was a quick learner. She recognized early in her career
that she needed to set herself apart from the other performers;
humor and daring became the means to achieve that goal. But
during this period she was still evolving. In her autobiography,
she said of this time in her career: "I was Mae West's toughest
audience. I needed new excitement, fresh inspiration." This
restless, ever-searching quality was to be a consistent trait in this
woman, who continued seeking new and better material long
after she had established herself as a superstar. In 1912, while
performing in Chicago, she went to the South Side to watch
some black dancers do a dance they called the "shimmy shawobble." The dancers arched their bodies and moved in a sensual manner. The next night, during her encore, West
introduced the shimmy to white audiences. Those who were not
scandalized (and maybe some of them, too) were delighted and
titillated by the daring moves of the shimmy. When she opened
at the Model Theater in Philadelphia later that year, the adver-
tisement read: "She does a muscle dance in a sitting position. It
is all in the way she does it, and her way is all her own."

The reviewers were not sure what to make of her. They were
already accustomed to Eva Tanguay's craziness and to Millie De
Leon's penchant for stripping on stage and kissing all of the men
in the audience, but they were not quite sure what Mae West
was all about. Sime Silverman of *Variety,* reviewing her act in

1912, said: "She's one of the many freak persons on the vaudeville stage where freakishness often carries more weight than talent, but Miss West should be coached to deliver the full value of her personality." Probably neither Silverman nor West really understood what the "full value" was at that point. Most of the theater managers were anxious to preserve vaudeville's reputation as family entertainment, yet they would not deny a popular entertainer a booking. One of West's many gags at the time was to wear a trick dress whose shoulder strap kept falling down, requiring her to make a conscious and dramatic effort to straighten it. She was warned by many managers to eliminate the trick, but each time she answered that she could not help it. The *Variety* reporter summed it up by saying: "The gal was always making a dress adjustment."

Audiences seemed to like her lewd gestures, her bold acrobatic dances, and her seemingly dirty lyrics. She often ended her act with the line: "It isn't what you do, it's how you do it." That seemed to sum up the audience's delight and the manager's dilemma. *Variety* in 1916 wrote: "She'll have to clean up her style—she has a way of putting dirty meanings in innocent lyrics." E. F. Albee, the boss of the vaudeville circuit operation, was known as a strait-laced man. The managers' complaints convinced him that Mae West should perform a song for him in his office so that he could see what all the fuss was about. According to her accompanist, Harry Richman:

> She had a line in her "Frankie and Johnny" number that went, "If you don't like my peaches, don't you shake my tree." She did this line as only Mae West could do it, and the men in the audience would scream and yell and go half-crazy. . . . When she did it for Albee, she clasped her hands close to one cheek and said it very clearly, almost childishly, and at the same time cast her eyes upward, the most mournful creature in the entire world. I nearly fell off my piano stool.

Albee did not understand what had caused such a commotion and Mae West returned to the vaudeville circuit.

Throughout the 1910s, Mae West moved toward the bawdy-woman genre of popular entertainment. The bawdy woman singer and dancer had been around in popular theaters for much of the nineteenth century. As America urbanized, as new immigrants came, as income levels went up, and as more men began attending popular theater, the audience for bawdiness continued to grow. Saloons, taverns, burlesque houses, and vaudeville shows all featured shady ladies who sang naughty lyrics. The dances were suggestive, the costumes were scanty, female modesty was forgotten, and the men laughed.

The bawdy women succeeded because their subject was sex and they used their facial expressions, their body language, the pacing and pausing of the words, and the timely wink of an eye to convey their message. Their flamboyant costumes also helped. Unlike circumspect respectable women, bawdy women paraded around the stage, boldly breaking the rules of ladylike behavior. Their willingness to "talk dirty," to express the forbidden in public, and to do it with great good humor defied conventionality and packed the theaters.

While owners of vaudeville theaters tried to maintain respectable standards, the cheers for the bawdy women far outweighed the boos. Stern moralists watched disapprovingly as bawdiness received popular acclaim. Bawdy women singers broke new ground in American entertainment. Although they never gained fame in such mass mainstream media as radio, the movies, or television, they secured a niche for themselves in Broadway theaters, vaudeville, and night clubs. Mae West became the exception by achieving fame in the movies as well.

The backgrounds of bawdy women performers varied. Most came from the working class, sometimes only a generation removed from immigrant origins. Mae West's mother had been born in Germany, Eva Tanguay came from French Canada, and Sophie Tucker's parents were Jewish immigrants from Russia. A few middle-class women performers overcame their family's disapproval to enter show business, but they were exceptions. Black bawdy singers usually came from poor rural families in the South; Moms Mabley came from Breward, North Carolina, and Bessie Smith came from Chattanooga, Tennessee.

Mae West's supremely self-confident personality fit right into the bawdy-woman mold. Although others wrote songs and comic skits for her, she began to revise all of her material and to write new songs for herself. She paid a lot of attention to the audience's reaction to every nuance, double entendre, wink, and gesture. Her costumes were elaborate and striking: tight-fitting black velvet dresses, seven-inch platform shoes, and a large hat cut out in the center to display her very blonde hair. Her swaying hips, guttural voice, flashing eyes, and diamond jewelry became established features of her act. When Mae West appeared, her fans knew what to expect; at the same time, they knew she would surprise them with more daring double entendres and new examples of her playful teases about love, romance, and sex.

During the war years 1914 to 1918, she continued to travel the vaudeville circuit. In 1915, she performed the first song she wrote on her own, "The Cave Girl." Dressed in a leopard-skin costume, West delighted her audience with the following lyrics:

> I got my smile from the sunshine;
> I got my tears from the rain;
> I learned to dance/When I saw the tiger prance.
> And the peacock taught me to be vain.
>
> A wise old owl in a tree so high
> He taught me how to wink my eye.
> I learned to bill and coo from a turtledove
> And a grizzly bear taught me how to hug.
>
> But the guy that lived two caves from me
> Taught me how to love.
> And that great, great Something from above
> Made us fall in love.

In 1916, Mae West played in an act with her sister, Beverly, something she had been resisting but agreed to in deference to her mother. Sime Silverman reviewed the act on July 10, 1916, and commented negatively on Mae's costume, a dinner jacket and silk top hat: "Perhaps if Miss West would wear men's dress altogether while upon the stage and stop talking, she would appear to better advantage. With 'sister' they could do a boy and girl 'sister' act." West agreed with Silverman's dissatisfaction with the sister act. She soon abandoned it to return to solo performing. Even at this early point in her career, she was unwilling to share the spotlight with anyone else, including her sister. In later years, Beverly lived at Mae's San Fernando Valley ranch and became her loyal supporter, but in these early years the relationship was strained and competitive. Mae West preferred to go it alone and receive all of the applause herself.

Audiences in the 1910s, particularly young men from both the working class and the college community, flocked to the vaudeville house to see her, staying through two shows in order to catch all her performances. The college men often unnerved the other entertainers when they left their reserved seats in the front rows empty until just minutes before West appeared. Then they ran down the aisles, upsetting the other members of the audience as well as the vaudevillians unfortunate enough to be appearing just before their idol. In New Haven, the Yale men screamed their delight with her lascivious smile, her throaty voice, her skin-tight costumes, and her assurance each night at the end of her act that "It's not what you do but how you do it" that counts. By most accounts, New Haven was Mae's town; no other vaudevillian came close to her popularity there.

Although she had appeared in some Broadway musicals earlier, West's first hit was in Arthur Hammerstein and Rudolf Friml's play *Sometime* in October 1918. Her second-act song, "Any Kind of Man," brought down the house. She also danced the shimmy shawobble, the first time Broadway audiences had seen her unique interpretation of the black dance. *Sometime* became the longest-running musical comedy of the season, 283 performances, lasting until June 1919. Mae West, ever restless for new places to exhibit her talent, developed a night-club show accompanied by the pianist Harry Richman.

Though the 1920s have the reputation as being bawdy and wild, many of these features were well in evidence in the previous decade. Risqué performers could be found in many places as show business flourished. Mae West had many compatriots on the Broadway stage as well as in vaudeville, burlesque houses, and night clubs. So-called sexual liberation, the questioning of sex roles, and the rise of feminism were publicly discussed subjects in pre–World War I America, in intellectual havens as well as in public entertainment houses. Women drinking alcohol in public, less modest dress and hairstyles, new occupations for women, and shrinking family size all seemed to suggest profound changes in the relations between the sexes. No one was clear about what these changes meant and whether they were temporary or permanent. Pundits offered their opinions in erudite and popular magazines.

One thing was clear, however: bawdy entertainers were smash hits. People paid to listen to Eva Tanguay screech her famous song, "I Don't Care," and West's shimmy attracted large audiences. Further, the mass-circulation newspapers gave free publicity to the performers. Pictures and interviews with them appeared regularly in the papers and weekly magazines.

After about 1910, night clubs became new and novel places for entertainment, particularly in big cities such as New York. Frequented mostly by the well-to-do, they offered expensive and intimate settings for shows, drinking, and dining. Sophie Tucker made this venue her home for more than fifty years. For Mae West, night clubs were successful stopping-off places in the early 1920s on the way to her next adventure. The intimacy of the night club offered performers the chance to be as bawdy as they wished. Subtlety was cast aside, and double entendres were replaced with outright ribaldry. Mae West, however, was dissatisfied with the small size of night club audiences, as well as with the noise, eating, drinking, and conversation during her act. In addition, vaudeville was losing popularity to silent films, and West no longer wished to endure the exhausting regimen of the vaudeville circuit. So the Broadway musical in the 1920s appeared to be the next best stage for her stylistic expressions. Although West did not abandon vaudeville and night clubs entirely at this point, the Broadway musical became her first choice.

As she continued to work on her stage persona, her public and private personalities merged. As the stage persona of Mae West gained popularity, she used the gestures, the witty one-liners, the brassy dress, and the swaggering walk in her everyday life as well. Soon the public and the private Mae West were one and the same. Indeed, she was to say of her greatest creation, Diamond Lil, "she's me and I'm her."

New Yorkers as well as nationwide readers of the new entertainment magazines became familiar with Mae West's face and figure. On December 25, 1919, she appeared on the cover of the New York *Dramatic Mirror,* and *Variety,* the national show business newspaper, reviewed her every appearance. The *Dramatic Mirror* called her a "Popular Broadway Comedienne." *Variety* reviewers, particularly *Variety* owner Sime Silverman, did not always approve of her off-color material. However, when she opened in a new show with Harry Richman in June 1922 at the Riverside Theater, *Variety's* review was filled with praise: "She rises to heights undreamed of for her and reveals unsuspected depths as a delineator of character songs, a dramatic reader of ability, and a girl with a flare for farce that will some day land her on the legitimate Olympus."

Although West's star was ascending in the 1920s, she still had to contend with a major competitor. While she was wowing audiences in night clubs in New York City in 1922, Eva Tanguay, the veteran vaudevillian, broke the Loew's State Theater record with a $29,000 take at fifty cents a ticket. This feat got Tanguay an engagement at the Palace Theater later in the season at a top ticket price of $3.00. This was a major accomplishment for a vaudevillian; such a steep price was usually reserved for a Broadway show. Surely she helped increase Mae West's aspirations.

Bigger is always better in entertainment circles and West was nothing if not competitive, always interested in increasing the size of her audience and her weekly salary. The successful components of her act, her image, and her public personality were already evident in the early 1920s, though they would undergo further revision and refinement during the decade. Her act included "character" songs, as the *Variety* review noted, a talent for delivering dramatic lines, a good sense of timing, an ability to cultivate the most absurd aspects of a comic situation, and sometimes a dance. Mae West was a true vaudevillian; she embraced the variety, the spectacle, the comedy, the music, and the costuming that characterized that entertainment form. Although she performed in night clubs with only a piano accompanist, her years in vaudeville and on the Broadway stage provided her with experience working with supporting players, an orchestra, and other acts. This experience would be invaluable during her Hollywood years.

As already suggested, successful women entertainers were a new breed in the 1920s. Few women in other professions could achieve the visibility and the influence of show business women. Although America had women teachers, lawyers, doctors, nurses, and scientists, they were in the minority and usually earned less money than their male counterparts. They were often single women whose earnings were needed to support themselves. But show business, which was a newly flourishing industry for both genders, offered women the potential to earn a lot of money, travel unchaperoned, dress in beautiful and flashy clothes, drive in the new motor cars, and experience adventure. Women performers in America had a unique opportunity to experience personal and economic independence. They earned their own money and could make decisions about their careers and how to spend that money without seeking male approval. Their identities, unlike the majority of American women, were based on their own accomplishments. American men, although they accepted the independence of women stars, never transferred that acceptance to their wives. Similarly, most American women assumed that their destiny in life was to be wives and mothers, although they admired their favorite women entertainers.

Mae West became very comfortable in the role of successful public person. She gladly granted interviews to reporters and proudly described her financial success. She was willing to discuss a wide range of subjects, although her private sexual exploits were not for public discussion. The many news accounts of her alleged amours were pure conjecture; they may have been based upon acquaintances' remarks and associates' speculations, but they were never accounts given by Mae West herself. It was, of course, her personal sexual exploits that most interested the press and the public. A major reason that women entertainers remained outside the mainstream of American life was their unconventional sexual behavior. Because their liaisons tended to be frequent and casual, many middle-class moralists viewed them as little better than prostitutes.

The special late-night world of show business came to be regarded with suspicion, and perhaps fear, by the general public. Particularly in the 1920s, the era of Prohibition, many entertainers mixed with gangsters, gamblers, dope dealers, and drinkers. Mae West's friendship with reputed mobster Owney Madden was widely publicized in the mid-1920s. Often, entertainers, gangsters, gamblers, and athletes came from the same neighborhoods and ethnic backgrounds. They sounded alike, shared the same attitudes, and enjoyed the same pleasures. The nasal Brooklyn twang never left Mae West's speech. She seemed content to display her origin and made no effort to mask it or to correct it.

Mae West neither apologized for nor defended her bawdy tastes and free-wheeling sexual values. Her interests blended nicely with those of the sporting, criminal, and entertainment worlds. All of those worlds were transient and full of uncertainty about the next booking or victory or caper. Although Mae West herself was abstemious, she liked the extravagant behavior of her compatriots. She may not have drunk with them or danced all night, but she liked to be around them for part of the evening and enjoyed her association with the bolder elements of society.

Paradoxically, some women entertainers held very conventional ideas about a woman's role, although they themselves led highly unconventional lives. They longed for marriage, home, family, and stability, even while engaging in casual sexual relationships. Such women looked upon their vaudeville experiences as temporary, youthful flings to be abandoned once they accumulated enough money or found a willing husband. But some women performers, particularly the bawdy women, relished their new-found freedom, fame, and independence. Those were the ones most feared by the censors. The bawdies believed in their risqué lyrics and practiced the freedom their songs and gestures portrayed.

Mae West was an inconsistent combination of both attitudes and behaviors. Although she did not smoke, drink, swear, or stay out all night (and she did not like her men to do any of these things either), she did believe in sexual freedom for women. She did not believe that marriage and family were woman's ultimate and only destiny. She herself remained unmarried and childless, she said, not because she was against family values, but rather because she was a star whose full-time occupations were self-development and self-promotion. A husband and children require time and attention that she could not spare from her career. This bald narcissism may have been declared and exhibited by some young flappers of the 1920s, but most of those very same women who danced the Charleston all night eventually dutifully married and became sedate housewives. Not Mae West. She enjoyed the life of an entertainer and a celebrity, and believed that she deserved all of the lavish attention that she received. She would never take up with a married man; that seemed to be her only moral guideline. Otherwise, if a man appealed to her and behaved like a gentleman, she enjoyed his company. As later discussions will show, she was more an individualist than a feminist, but her often-quoted remarks about women's rights could be applied by feminists as evidence of her support. West, however, never joined any women's organizations nor, by her own admission, did she enjoy the company of women. Still, her declarations of sexual freedom rang a responsive chord in the hearts of 1920s liberals.

As Mae West's fame increased, so did her public enjoyment of her favorite pastimes. West was particularly attracted, for example, to prize fighters. She admired tall, burly, muscular men who towered over her. (West's height, like many things about her, is a matter of dispute. Some accounts state that she was barely five feet tall, thus explaining the seven-inch platform shoes observers always commented on; other sources indicate that she was five feet, five inches tall. Most photographs support the five-feet view; she is usually pictured looking up at a man who appears to be at least a foot taller.) West frequented boxing matches and socialized with such heavyweight champions as James J. Corbett and Jack Dempsey. West always valued publicity, and she quickly realized that photographers would scramble to get a picture of a champion fighter and a popular vaudevillian.

In addition to capitalizing on the celebrity of her muscular companions, West was also adding another dimension to her personality: that of the sexpot who admired well-built men as much as they admired well-built women. The image of a sexually active woman who saw no difference between her needs and preferences and those of men became an integral part of the Mae West persona. West, an astute observer of modern media, appreciated the fact that frequent mention of her in the newspapers and magazines of the day helped ticket sales to her shows. A typical picture of Mae West, and there are hundreds of them from 1910 through the 1960s, shows her smiling slyly as she feels the bulging biceps of a grinning muscle man. In the 1950s muscle men would become an integral part of her night club act.

Pictures of her with different men, sometimes surrounded by many men, all looking admiringly at her, added to the Mae West mystique. If one man was good, two were better, and three still better. Her pictures affirmed her appreciation of numerous men, one succeeding another, and featured her as the sole female, the star in the center of the universe. In a period when women were expected to be monogamous, loyal to the one true love of their life, Mae West offered an exciting fantasy. Although few women imitated her lifestyle, many may have secretly dreamed about her exciting life. And men fans enjoyed the obvious pleasure she took in life. Rather than feeling threatened by her sexual exploits, they seemed to delight in her audacity. Men enjoyed good-time gals, and Mae West was the best of them. Her male friends often became her confidants and companions; West seemed to enjoy, both in private and in public, constant male attention. Women, however, she found superfluous.

According to her own account, Mae West cherished her independence and freedom; she never wished to lean on a man. Although this trait appealed to her male fans—they could fantasize about a good time with Mae while certain that their wives were home dutifully awaiting their return—it caused problems with some of the men in her private life. Only those who found her spunky independence attractive could maintain a relationship with her. For men who wished a no-strings-attached relationship, Mae West was the woman to know, in fact or in fantasy. Her desire for sexual experiences with many different partners, she claimed, was a natural urge of the species. That she indulged in it without guilt or remorse made her different from the majority of American men and women. But West believed that both genders shared her desire, although few women had the opportunity, without risking their respectability, to act on it. In interviews throughout her career, as well as in her 1959 autobiography, *Goodness Had Nothing to Do With It,* she expounded this viewpoint. She practiced what she preached.

Such interest in sex and self-absorption were socially acceptable traits in men, but not in women. Ambitious, selfish men could have families and careers, and in fact were admired; ambitious women were to be feared and, preferably, crushed. Her personal declarations were subversive, yet she presented them with great humor and fostered the view that her behavior and her personality were unique; she did not consider herself a social threat since she was one of a kind.

Mae West's obvious ambition was such a departure from the norm for women that it became an asset rather than a deficit. By

the early 1920s, she was a one-woman industry, zealously cultivating her image as an insatiable sex comic. Her atypicality, in
lifestyle and message, certainly did give her a unique position in
show business.

To recapture the flavor and the specifics of the performances of
eighty years ago, it is necessary to rely on contemporary memoirs, reviewers' assessments, and reporters' descriptions of the
acts. After all, vaudeville ended its long, successful run in the
early 1930s, when its remnants served as the live entertainment
portion of the program offered in a new movie palace. The
headliners from vaudeville sometimes made a successful transition to radio or the movies, but most left show business altogether. Eva Tanguay retired, as did Millie De Leon. Mae West
moved on to Broadway and then to the movies, but she kept her
hand in live performance by making personal appearances
around the country on the stages of the various Paramount theaters where her movies were playing.

Variety, the show business newspaper, sent reporters to cover
the new acts of leading vaudevillians, the Broadway musicals,
and night club acts. Sime Silverman, the founder and chief reporter of *Variety,* often reviewed Eva Tanguay's and Mae West's
acts himself. Local newspapers also sent reporters to cover the
entertainments of the city. It was a sign of the growing importance of show business that most newspapers, after 1910, had entertainment sections and reporters assigned to that beat. In 1915,
for example, a reporter for the St. Louis *Globe-Democrat* described for his readers a show in which Millie De Leon (considered an Eva Tanguay imitator by her critics and a fresh original
by her admirers) jumped into the aisles and kissed many different men until she had "left the imprint of her vermilion lips on
the forehead of a dozen or more. Then oblivion."

Only eyewitness accounts can provide such juicy details. Another reporter commented that Eva Tanguay's costumes "actually possess a sense of humor themselves." In a New York *Post*
clipping from July 8, 1909, we learn that Millie De Leon was

charged with being a public nuisance after a performance of the
Salomé dance. When she asked the three justices before whom
she stood for permission to demonstrate her version of the
dance, she was refused. She insisted that she could not have performed the dance as her accusers said, with wriggles, because
the costume weighed eighty-five pounds. "My dance," she was
quoted as saying, "is a pure Salomé dance, the real thing. Just
such a dance as Eva Tanguay and Gertrude Hoffman give. The
act itself is nothing but comedy, absolutely nothing indecent,
and everybody laughs at its conclusion." De Leon's spirit, and
her frequent trips before the judges, were duly reported in the
newspapers, which attested to her popularity and her news-
worthiness.

Public officials did not share Mae West's sense of humor. De
Leon, Tanguay, Hoffman, Tucker, and West were often hauled
before judges for public indecency or corrupting the morals of
minors. Newspapers covered every arrest and appearance in
court, and although people may have nodded their approval of
the police's vigilance, the entertainers usually got off with a sus-
pended sentence or a fine, and audiences flocked to their next
performance. In the 1920s, Mae West received a jail term for appearing in a Broadway play she had written called *Sex* (see chapter 2). The vaudevillians kept on daring the police and censors
to arrest them, the police obliged, and the entertainers blithely
continued to perform. The free publicity only increased the size
of the audiences. But the tension between public taste and
bawdy excesses continued through the 1920s and was later transferred to Hollywood.

Taken together, the reports and the remembrances provide
the foundation for all re-creations of Mae West's career as well
as the show business atmosphere of vaudeville's heyday. Although we can watch most of Mae West's movies of the 1930s, we
have no audio or video record of her vaudeville acts or her
Broadway plays; we cannot see the gestures, the timing, and the
wink that established her reputation. We must rely on written
reports, witnesses' accounts, the original scripts, and second-

and third-hand stories. The fragility of memory, the concern for self-enhancement, the improvisations on stage, and the power of performers all must be considered, but ultimately cannot be evaluated. The Mae West persona described herein relies largely on literary sources; both the writer and the reader must keep this fact in mind.

CHAPTER TWO

She Went Up the Ladder of Success, Wrong by Wrong

1923–1932

Live entertainment still attracted large audiences in the 1920s. People found prosperity with the end of the Great War and were ready to spend money on amusements. As one journal reported in December 1920, "The general demand for amusements that followed the ending of the war has increased in the matter of theatres." Although the economic boom that accompanied the end of war in 1919 did not affect all Americans equally, urban dwellers found their wages rising, as did the growing middle class. More and more urban Americans found work in the new offices and stores. Young people in particular spent money and energy on personal pleasure, not unlike recent times. Advocates of women's suffrage, for example, found the new generation of women less interested in reform and more interested in dancing all night.

The popular image of the "roaring twenties," though hardly representative of life for all Americans in that decade, surely applied to a significant portion of the middle and upper classes, white and black. Harlem, the growing black ghetto of New York, attracted both races to its famous night clubs. Indeed, only whites were allowed to patronize the Cotton Club, a well-known jazz club that featured black entertainers. Jazz music, the creation of black musicians, swept the country, and audiences, both black and white, listened and danced to the new music. Night clubs prospered during Prohibition, serving illegal liquor in teacups.

On Broadway, musicals predominated, with ticket prices running as high as twelve dollars, a great deal of money at the time. Some were musical comedies, a particularly American adaptation of the European operetta; others were revues. But all musicals emphasized the songs and the singers, and were far less concerned with the plot. Between 1921 and 1924, there were 120 musicals in town, with half being musical comedy. Many of the leading vaudevillians transferred their skills from the fading vaudeville houses to the still-vibrant Broadway stage. Blanche Ring, May Irwin, and Mae West all appeared in live theater during the period. West, as usual, found herself surrounded by lots of competitors, ambitious women performers who were willing to do almost anything to attract an audience.

The vaudeville theaters, in an effort to remain alive, introduced reserved seats, much like the Broadway theaters and the new picture shows. Eva Tanguay still attracted standing-room-only crowds, assuring her $3,500 a week salary. The optimism of the period enabled impresario Florenz Ziegfeld to mount his most ambitious show to date in 1921. The Ziegfeld Follies of that year cost a quarter of a million dollars to produce and included scenes recreating the Royal Gardens of Versailles as well as a twelfth-century Persian palace. The show also featured the comedy of W. C. Fields and Bert Williams and Fanny Brice singing her soon-to-become famous rendition of "My Man." As one entertainment historian noted: "Until sound films lured many of the best entertainers to Hollywood, Broadway offered a variety of great performers unmatched before or since."

Mae West had a lot of company at the bawdy end of the performing spectrum. Blanche Ring, who appeared in the Shubert musical revue *The Passing Show of 1919* at the Winter Garden in New York, was known as a red-hot mamma. Some of the bawdy singers also displayed comic talent. Charlote Greenwood appeared in musical revues during the 1920s, performing comic songs as well as self-deprecating skits. In the fall of 1919, West joined producer Ned Wayburn's variety company, which performed in New York's Capitol Theater, as the resident comedienne.

The more traditional images of women could still be seen on the stage. The "Dumb Dora" type, the stereotype of the sweet but dim-witted woman, gained a lot of currency during the decade, and the naive innocent type, who needed a man to protect her, was often seen in the melodramas. In all of these vehicles, the audience did not seem to demand high-quality plots. They were mainly interested in seeing their star presented in a favorable light. The musical comedy stars, for example, sang their favorite and most popular songs in all of their plays, whether they were relevant to the story or not. As Blanche Ring said, the plots were merely "something to hang songs on." Although critics lamented the low quality of the theater fare, the audiences kept coming. Neither the moralists nor the elitist critics could convince theatergoers that they should demand higher standards of their favorite performers.

Mae West was an astute observer and participant in this scene. She displayed her perfectionistic streak by searching for new and better material. Novelty was the key as she sought to set herself off from the other performers and assure enduring success. Her personal style, though still evolving, already exhibited clearly identifiable traits: the familiar tight-fitting velvet dress aglitter with rhinestones, the diamond rings and bracelets that loaded her hands, the blonde hair puffed up on top of her head, and her smiling eyes that invited men to enjoy the view. She exuded self-satisfaction and good humor. Mae West knew that she was selling herself; the major product—indeed, the only product—was her personality. If she could create an enduring audience, her future and her star status were assured. A comic perspective and risqué material seemed to be a winning combination.

West sang every song with a laugh and a leer; every dance emphasized her interest in sex. She considered herself an actress who sang and danced. This perspective was important, as it affected how she presented herself to her audience and played a major role in the direction her career took. Mae West claimed that her dramatic potential had not been fully realized on the vaudeville stage and she needed new outlets for her talent. Because she was very ambitious and focused on her own success, she was willing to experiment, picking and choosing ideas, gestures, and formats from any and all environments.

Mae West was not a conventional beauty, so she had to figure out a way to maximize her assets and use her seeming deficits to best advantage. Her facial features were not delicate, so she exaggerated them with makeup and gestures. Her eyes were small, but she opened them wide and exuded sheer confidence in her desirability. She dressed in a way that flaunted her full bosom and hips, wearing a special corset to accentuate them further. She enjoyed the styles of the 1890s, which emphasized women's bodices and bustles.

In the early 1920s, Mae West appeared in vaudeville shows as well as Broadway musicals and night clubs, but she found no takers among the big time Broadway producers for her style and personality. The Shuberts, Charles Dillingham, and Flo Ziegfeld, for example, considered their plays high toned and respectable, while Mae West was already known for her bawdy style. Since she did not want to descend into burlesque or continue on the exhausting vaudeville circuit, she had to find a suitable vehicle, one that would allow her to be the good-time bad girl she loved to portray. She also had to win the approval of a mainstream audience, or at least the larger audience that frequented Broadway. She had already written many songs and routines for herself; West claimed that she jotted down ideas for plays all of the time. People walking on the street, overheard conversations, the plots of successful Broadway shows—all were grist for her creative mill.

West knew that plays with sexual content were greeted by good ticket sales, heavy media coverage, and threats that they would be closed down. Although politicians always agreed with the moralists that bawdy plays had no place on Broadway, they turned a deaf ear when discussions shifted to legal censorship. After all, the theater was big business in New York, and no politician wanted to be held responsible for economic depressions in the city. The newspapers, however, paid lip service to the moral censors. One account, denying that Broadway was filled with filth, conceded that there was an audience for shady plays: "Its patrons come from out of town, in the main—gay dogs from upstate and from 'the sticks,' looking for a fling of wickedness in a supposedly wicked city." Such accounts did not explain the large numbers of New Yorkers who regularly attended such plays.

In May 1923, Sholem Asch's play *The God of Vengeance,* about a Polish brothel keeper and his daughter, was considered immoral and the whole cast was arrested at the instigation of the New York Anti-Vice Society. Indeed, there were citizen review groups who attended Broadway plays and pointed out to the police any they considered an affront to public decency. The fear of censorship, backed by stringent state laws, was a constant threat to Broadway's mainstream producers. To Mae West, the publicity attending the closing down of a show might be worth the cost of being shut down. Bad publicity, like good publicity, sparked public interest.

West's future struggles with censors added her name to a long list of people who defied majority values. The idea of citizen or legally mandated censorship of artistic and commercial entertainments has had a long history in America. One reason for restraining expression that has existed since the colonial Puritans outlawed theatrical productions in early America was the moral one: the belief that frivolous entertainment and drama of questionable morality hurt the moral development of the citizenry. The church elders or the secular authorities in these cases assumed that they knew what was good for people and that they, as community leaders, had the right and obligation to impose their views. By 1910, a new, large immigrant population was beginning to add another dimension to the censorship theme: the view that these unruly masses had to be acculturated and that exposure to material of dubious social value would hinder, if not halt, the process. For all of these reasons, and because the theaters, burlesque, vaudeville, and the new silent films seemed to appeal to the lowest common denominator, the censors organized and tried to control what they saw as anarchic, dangerous, and socially irresponsible material on America's stages.

They also were alarmed by the flagrant violation of Prohibition in the new night clubs, where illegally obtained liquor was served in teacups. Bootleggers, who secretly distributed alcohol throughout the country, prospered, undeterred by the legal authorities. Organized crime grew, and gangland violence became a new feature on the urban landscape. In this atmosphere, censorship of entertainment material was understandable. If liquor was injurious to your personal conduct and the well-being of your family, as moralists claimed, then the same logic argued that viewing a play with immoral or sexual connotations would positively corrupt you. Censors and their supporters believed that people were easily influenced by suggestive material. Because the censors held a dim view of peoples' ability to judge for themselves, they called for government bodies and citizen review boards to supervise plays, vaudeville acts, radio programs, and later the movies.

Although censors had very limited success on Broadway and in America's bookstores, they were to enjoy much more control over movies, the radio, and eventually television. They were particularly concerned with impressionable youth, who they believed could not distinguish fact from fiction, fantasy from reality. Mae West struggled with censorship throughout the 1920s and 1930s, as did many other entertainers. No wonder they spoke out for freedom of speech and assembly; their very livelihood was jeopardized by censorship.

During this period of searching for new material and a new venue, Mae West became associated with James Timony, a lawyer who had handled some business affairs for her mother. This association, which was both personal and professional, would last until Timony died in 1954. His legal talents would be very important to West, in terms of the various contracts she entered into as well as the numerous lawsuits in which she defended herself. Timony was very loyal to her and always protected her interests. He advised her on all of her projects and she came to rely upon his judgment.

In 1925, Mae West was thirty-two years old, already over the hill by some show business standards. She could no longer play the ingenue, nor did she wish to. Her image as an alluring, sexy woman seemed hackneyed and overdone to her critics, who found her predictable and old hat. Her challenge was to take the stereotyped image she projected, that of the naughty girl with a sense of humor, and make it uniquely her own. Her figure was not fashionable in the flapper 1920s when the unisex look prevailed; further, she had lots of competition as the whore with a heart of gold. Ever ambitious and self-confident, she intensified her search for the right play.

West could not imagine a life without a public or a life without a stage. Unwilling to travel on the vaudeville circuit any longer and unable to break into a "respectable" Broadway musical, West began writing a play in which she could star. She already had confidence in her ability to alter other peoples' songs and skits to suit her personality. Why not create her own vehicle? This interest in shaping material to her particular style would characterize all of her work, with very few exceptions, for the remainder of her career. In 1925, under the pen name Jane Mast, she wrote a play that guaranteed her headlines. The play was called *Sex,* a title that ensured notoreity. This was the only time West used a pseudonym; she wanted to test the waters before accepting responsibility for the play.

Sex opened at Daly's Theater in New York City on April 26, 1926. West, Timony, and other investors who believed in her brand of humor rented the theater and mounted the production on their own. The New York *Herald Tribune* critic said that it "wins high marks for depravity (and) dullness...." The *New York Times* critic said that in the first act, there were oohs and ahs from the audience, and "except for a torrid love scene toward the end it contented itself with just being pretty feeble and disjointed." Bob Sisk, the *Variety* reporter, observed that "...the third act played to lots of empty seats....Mae West plays the rough gal, and in the first act does it well. But she goes to pieces after that, because she doesn't change when the play calls for it...." The play's dullness confounded audiences, who went to the theater prepared to be shocked; however, audiences kept coming.

The story line of *Sex* sounds like a grade-B movie or a third-rate television melodrama. West starred as Margie LaMont, a Montreal prostitute who followed the British fleet from port to port. The plot involved blackmail, kidnapping (of an innocent society woman, not world-weary Margie), Margie's seduction of a society youth, and, finally, her departure to follow the fleet again. The story took more turns than a roller coaster. But Margie always remained kind-natured, cynical but not sour, and a good sport who understood human nature better than most. When she helps the society woman escape from the evil clutches of a blackmailer, she is accused by the woman of being part of the plot. In revenge, Margie seduces the society woman's son. She lures him to the altar but she does not go through with the marriage. She is, after all, a "bad" girl with a heart of gold and realizes that because she is a shady lady by profession, she cannot win the rich guy. Being philosophical, another characteristic of a good-hearted whore, she accepts her fate and returns to her occupation.

This play, like West's subsequent ones, defied convention, not only in terms of subject matter, but also in terms of form. Though seemingly a melodrama, a slice-of-life drama about the underworld, it also borrowed elements from the musical, with West offering songs that were unrelated to the plot line. This mixing of genres became a regular feature of West's future plays. One reason the critics did not respond favorably to her plays, perhaps, is because they were not sure whether they were melodramas or comedies or musicals. If asked, West might have replied that they were a little bit of all three. West did not believe in discarding assets: her singing and her sashaying were just that and they had to be incorporated into all of her work.

The stereotype of Eve, the bad girl, was common in Broadway plays, novels, and silent films. Mae West's major contribution to the image was to make Eve an initiator of actions rather than the victim of circumstances. In contrast to Theodore Dreiser's *Sister Carrie* and its many imitators, Mae West's Margie LaMont and, later, Diamond Lil were take-charge women. Their danger to contemporary values was muted because they lived in the past. Thus audiences could admire the audacity of Margie and Lil while feeling removed from them. Both men and women laughed at her wisecracks, watched her uncomplaining behavior, and applauded her at the end. Whereas most prostitutes died at the end of the melodrama, West's whores always remained very much alive. They may not have won the rich guy, but they won their independence.

Most New York newspapers would not print ads for a play titled *Sex,* though some relented; respectable folk stayed away from the Daly Theater but many others, locals as well as out-of-towners, came. The rowdier element among working men turned out in great number and helped to make the play a financial success. West estimated that the audience was usually only 20 percent female, and she tried to increase the appeal to women by softening the coarser features of the story. It is not clear whether she succeeded. She knew that the title was controversial and that it would attract more men than women, but she reveled in the publicity and used it to remind her fans that sex was part of life, indeed a very pleasant part.

West and James Timony were sensitive to the charge that their play appealed only to men's baser instincts. They defended *Sex,* claiming that women would find it a good theatrical experience as well. West's appearance on Broadway, she believed, could be the beginning of her rise to respectability, of status in the profession. If *Sex* only appealed to rowdy men, Mae West would be accused of bringing burlesque to Broadway, a charge that was leveled at many actors.

In *Sex* and in her subsequent plays, West explored the forbidden world of criminals, gamblers, waterfront gangs, and other groups with dubious standing in society. She seemed to relish the opportunity to bring to a respectable Broadway audience's attention the doings of a portion of society unknown to them. She responded to the "slumming" instinct of middle-class people. She depicted society's outcasts very sympathetically in her plays. The high-society types were portrayed as cold, unfeeling snobs; the underworld figures, by contrast, were real people with real problems, adventures, and emotions. Not only did she suggest that sex drove most people to both good and bad results, but also that all forbidden subjects deserved a public airing, a decidedly subversive idea.

While the censors wanted the play closed, the more politically minded police chief stood warily by, unsure of what, if anything, he should do; meanwhile, the play ran for 375 performances. Then, while Mayor Jimmy Walker (a theater aficionado) was on vacation, the ambitious acting mayor decided to do the "righteous" thing: he ordered a raid on *Sex* and two other Broadway plays with controversial story lines. The other two plays, *The Captive* and *The Virgin Man,* also were closed down. The police action came nearly a year after the plays had opened and had been passed over by the play jury of the New York County district attorney's office. Many observers were puzzled by the police's behavior. Some blamed an ambitious acting mayor, others claimed that West's next play, *The Drag,* already in preview performances in New Jersey, was so shocking that *Sex* was closed down to prevent it from opening in New York. If so, the strategy worked.

The New York newspapers and magazines had a field day with Mae West's arrest. While many observers advocated aesthetically superior plays and morally uplifting fare, they also abhorred censorship. "The way to overcome evil is not by suppressing or trying to prohibit it, but rather by making good more attractive," said one newspaper. "Once the general standard of discrimination has been elevated by means of better plays, there will be no profitable market for salacious ones." Many wondered why a play that had been deemed harmless to public morality one year before became objectionable the next year. A number of reviewers noted that *The Virgin Man* had been about to close when its cast was arrested. The demand for tickets then became so overwhelming that the producers extended the run for another three weeks.

During the furor over censorship, Mayor Jimmy Walker, known as a friend of show business, gave a speech on April 2, 1927, in which he pledged to do what he could to uphold purity in the theater. "And let me say right now that there will never be a censorship of the stage as long as I can help it; censorship is un-American. When any alleged entertainment in this city becomes a stench to the nostrils, then we don't need a censor. What we need is a good loud blast on the police whistle." Walker's position, a popular one among entertainers of course, walked the fine line of upholding morality while advocating free expression, a delicate and politically astute position. It was the audience that would determine public taste, and the idealists hoped that it could be educated to higher levels of amusement. If a law was broken, then the guilty would be prosecuted but freedom of expression required just that.

Meanwhile, in April 1927, Mae West, Jim Timony, and Clarence Morganstern, the manager, were charged with corrupting the morals of youth. During the trial, a publicity extravaganza for West, the police chief was hard-pressed to point to obscene words, lines, or actions. Finally, he claimed that West's personality, along with a belly dance she performed, were the sources of the immorality. During this testimony, West asked the judge for permission to demonstrate the dance to the court, which he granted. West performed the dance wearing a tight metallic evening gown. As she described it:

The prosecutor questioned one of the arresting officers in detail about this dance. The officer blushed and testified, "Miss West moved her navel up and down and from right to left."

"Did you actually see her navel?" my lawyer asked him.

"No, but I saw something in her middle that moved from east to west."

The courtroom roared.

Despite the obvious good humor in the courtroom, West, Timony, and Morganstern were convicted. West was fined $500 and sentenced to ten days in the Welfare Island prison. Her drive to jail, her daily bulletins from her cell, and her release after eight days (two days off for good behavior) all received loving attention in the press. Timony and Morganstern each got ten-day sentences.

The *Police Gazette* reporter noted that West took her incarceration philosophically, saying "she would improve her time in the 'hoosegow' by gathering material for another play." The eight days in jail, she said, did not change her. "I still believe I am innocent, and that my play was not offensive. It has cost me $50 a day to live at Welfare Island, but all in all it was worth it." She later told an interviewer the publicity she received "was worth a million dollars." Mae West wrote an article about her prison experience for *Liberty* magazine. She was paid $1,000, which she donated to the prison library, which she said was "antiquated and small. It was one of my duties to dust it, so I know." West also said she was going to try to get jobs for some of the women recently released from the jail, as they were penniless. No newspaper reporter followed up on this story.

She also told reporters that she was planning to take *Sex* to Chicago. As West later explained her success in *Sex:*

Everyone wants to write plays about a man 'n' woman or men 'n' men. But my style is a woman among men—just the reverse of what's always been written, see? I found I showed to the greatest advantage when I kept the other parts straight and exaggerated my own.

This style—"a woman among men"—established a pattern that would be followed in all of her subsequent plays. West and her sexual needs were the center of attention. By presenting the material humorously, by hamming it up, West was able to dissipate the controversy, mute the social implications of her words and actions, and allow everyone to have a good time. By emphasizing her enormous egocentricity, she shocked and delighted her fans with her audacity. Could anyone actually be so self-centered? When discussing Mae West, the answer was always in the affirmative.

Mae West needed Jim Timony's lawyerly advice during this period. Former associates who claimed that she had stolen their material were suing her. This problem was to dog her throughout her career: West always insisted upon sole writing credit for all of her plays as well as for the movie scripts she later wrote in Hollywood even when others contributed. Although she eventually relented and allowed some other names to be credited on the silver screen, during her Broadway years, in the late 1920s, she always insisted upon exclusive credit. Since she did use other writers' stories and ideas, the result was many lawsuits, which she usually won, but which required her time and her money. Of course, she used the publicity that accompanied all of this litigation to her benefit. West thought that getting your name and picture in the newspaper was always a positive thing, no matter the reason.

The Drag, her second foray into play writing, was a play based upon an even more sensational subject: homosexuality. West knew many male homosexuals in the theater. Indeed, while still in vaudeville she had been influenced by the style, gestures, and costumes of such famous female impersonators as Julian Eltinge and, especially, Bert Savoy. She used the same writer as Savoy in those days, Thomas J. Gray, and frequently watched Savoy perform. His red wig, bejewelled fingers, fancy garters, and slit skirts impressed her. In one Savoy skit, he looked his partner, Jay Brennan, up and down slowly, dangled his hotel keys, and remarked: "Oh, you're lonesome, huh? Well, it's your own fault!'' Mae West was to incorporate the gesture and, with some alteration, the lines, in her future numbers.

Throughout this century, female impersonators have had an audience. The novelty of seeing slim-hipped, clean-shaven men with feminine features dress as women and imitate female gestures and speech patterns has fascinated audiences of both genders. Male homosexuals have been the biggest fans of female impersonators, but heterosexual men and women also attended Eltinge's and Savoy's performances. Indeed, Eltinge and Savoy were regularly reviewed in the theatrical columns of New York newspapers. The sheer audacity of such a spectacle awed and delighted many. The complex psychological reasons for the fascination were not explored. Both Eltinge and Savoy were pretty men who could look like pretty women.

Savoy was an admitted homosexual, as were many members of his audience. A number of them were entertainers, set designers, choreographers, and writers working in New York's rich and diverse theatrical world. Female impersonators performed for their cohorts as well as for the middle and upper class heterosexual audiences who were curious about this phenomenon. Cross dressing both excited homosexual audiences and satisfied their need for novelty, their secret wish to wear flamboyant clothes of the opposite sex, and their desire to assume female characteristics. Women fans may have marvelled at the style, the bravado, and the dash of these female impersonators, most of whom were also talented singers, dancers, and mimics.

Mae West herself was accused of being a female impersonator by many befuddled critics of the day—she seemed to be such an exaggeration of female behavior and the female form. West shared with female impersonators and homosexuals an interest in ribaldry, in extreme dress and behavior, and in satirizing social attitudes toward sex. The blurring of the lines between men and women also appealed to her. The very willingness to consider that which is surprising, as she noted, assured box-office success.

West admired the courage of the female impersonators and enjoyed their company and their affected feminine style. They, in turn, were among her most ardent fans. They admired her broad, bawdy approach to sexual matters, and they laughed with her when she was accused of being a female impersonator. The sincere admiration that many gay men had for her pleased her. Without being preachy, she brought to the public's attention a topic that had always been kept behind closed doors. Although she held the conventional attitude that homosexuality was an illness rather than a healthy alternative, her tolerance of human differences as well as her commonsensical approach to life demanded respectful treatment of all groups in society, including homosexuals.

Because homosexuality was a forbidden subject, and therefore would receive a lot of attention, Mae West decided to write about it but in her own inimitable style. Although her play pretended to be a serious drama, intent upon treating the subject as a medical problem, it actually was raucous and violent. *The Drag* concerned an aristocratic man, Rolly Kingsbury, who hid his homosexuality from his prominent family. He married, only to make the young woman miserable and bewildered about her husband's unwillingness to consummate the marriage. Rolly continued to consort with his gay friends and to try to seduce attractive heterosexual men. He was killed in the third act by a rejected lover. The lurid plot assured controversy.

There were two particularly shocking scenes in *The Drag,* according to the few critics who saw the play. In one, Rolly Kingsbury made a pass at a heterosexual man; in the other, there was a huge drag ball where forty homosexuals sang, danced, and conversed. West said of the scene: "It was the oddest party ever produced on an American stage during a serious drama." Witnesses were so preoccupied with the sensational nature of the material that few noted the dramatic or comedic material, if there was any, in the play. The underground world of the gay community had never been depicted in this way on the Broadway stage. Serious dramas about homosexuality, such as *The*

Captive had been performed, but never such a raw and raucous play. West's daring and sheer grit, however, seemed to be a successful formula.

"Was I a crusader?" she asked rhetorically in her 1959 autobiography. No, she answered, her interest was in exposing the hypocrisy of those who attended the controversial plays and afterwards preached against them. West also argued that gay men were women inside male bodies and they deserved society's sympathy. Further, she argued, in the privacy of one's bedroom, one should be free to do whatever one wishes, as long as no one was hurt and no children were involved. *The Drag* opened in Bridgeport, Connecticut, at the Park Theater on January 31, 1927. It also played in Paterson, New Jersey, to sold-out audiences. But when it came time to bring *The Drag* to New York, Timony was advised, for legal reasons, not to do so. After the experience with *Sex,* he knew what would be in store for the principals in *The Drag.* Reluctantly, West agreed not to bring the show to New York.

West's desire to bring the forbidden and seamy sides of life to respectable New Yorkers was based on both a liberal's interest in free expression and an interest in commercial success. The positive publicity that resulted from the legal troubles of *The Drag* had already been reaped. She was still fighting the charges regarding *Sex,* and she did not care to be involved in yet another lengthy legal battle. West's personality enjoyed a good fight, but her practical nature told her when to cut her losses and move on to the next project. She had infinite confidence in her ability to write new and better plays. Despite its limited out-of-town run, *The Drag* had made money and assured West of an audience for her next play.

West's fans did not have to wait long. Her third theatrical production was called *The Wicked Age.* Although the title promised more of the salacious material now associated with Mae West, the comedy concerned an exposé of bathing beauty contests, hardly a juicy enough subject for sensation-seeking audiences. West played the leading role of Evelyn Carson. *The Wicked*

Age previewed in New Haven, where the Yale men loyally attended the latest West offering. But the New Haven *Journal-
Courier* was not as generous. They found it "devoid of any
merit." *The Wicked Age* opened on November 4, 1927, in New
York at Daly's Theater. The play was well received by the audience, though the critics considered it light fare. The *New York
Times* critic said it was mild compared to *Sex* and would not require the presence of the police. But he also called it "the low
point of the theatrical season," and complained that it was very
long, going on until midnight. He concluded by saying that *The
Wicked Age* was "incredibly cheap and vulgar trash, with only
such minor amusement as was to be derived from watching the
exhibitionistic antics of Miss West as a faintly redeeming feature."

In addition to poor reviews, West had problems with her leading man. She found him inept and unable to project his voice
beyond the first few rows. Although she offered to pay his salary
for the run of the show if he would leave, he refused, and negotiations with Actors Equity did not end satisfactorily. West
claimed that she closed the show after nineteen performances
rather than continue with him. In fact, poor ticket sales may
have prompted her action as well. In her autobiography, she insisted that her perfectionistic streak governed her action. "I
have never asked for second chances," she wrote. She demanded
a great deal of herself and expected all of her colleagues to do
likewise.

The next play that Mae West wrote gave her the fictional
character that became the basis for her superstar image—
Diamond Lil. It was first performed in Brooklyn at Teller's Shubert Theater on April 4, 1928, prior to its Manhattan opening
on April 9th at the Royale Theater. The title role embraced all of
the characteristics West had been cultivating since her early days
in vaudeville. Lil was a whore with a heart of gold. Spouting a
string of one-liners and sporting a leering smile to match that of
any male Lothario's, Lil became the public personality that
merged with the private West. West was to say repeatedly, "Dia-

mond Lil is me and I'm her and there ain't no difference." Lil combined a sense of humor with a no-nonsense approach to sexual matters. The play allowed West to exhibit her funny and exaggerated qualities in a better developed character and a more substantial plot than in her earlier efforts. *Diamond Lil* ran for 176 performances and then went on tour. It was to be a successful road show the first time out as well as in frequent revivals that would continue for the next thirty years.

Diamond Lil is set in a dance hall in the Bowery in the 1890s. Gangsters from the underworld are mixed in with the regular drinking crowd. The Dance hall girls sell their services, both on the dance floor and in the rooms above. Diamond Lil had earned her way to the top of this shady world by being the best saleswoman around. She sported diamonds up and down both arms and slept in a huge wooden bed shaped like a swan. Indeed, at the opening of the second act, she lounged in the swan bed reading a copy of the *Police Gazette*. She later sang the highly suggestive ballad "Frankie and Johnny." Lil was always surrounded by male admirers, all competing for her attention. In one scene, when an admirer said, "your hands, your lips, your hair, your magnificent shoulder," she interrupted him, asking: "What're you doin' honey? Making love or takin' inventory?"

Lil became interested in the only man around who was decidedly uninterested in her—at least in the way that she wished. He was a Salvation Army officer intent on converting her to the righteous path. It was in a scene with him that West uttered what would become one of her most famous lines: "Come up and see me some time." She also said, "You can be had," a line that was received negatively by the censors of the day. Lil wished no change in her life; she only wanted to continue to have fun, which she did to everyone's delight. The critics joined the audiences in proclaiming *Diamond Lil* to be a first-class amusement. The acclaim established Mae West's status as a superstar.

The *New York Times* critic loved *Diamond Lil*. For the first time, that august newspaper's writer found West's acting to be superb, though the writing of the play was considered "to be a bit thick." Her overall performance, particularly her attitude toward sex, he found "almost Elizabethan," that is to say, bawdy. *Diamond Lil* had a good supporting cast of characters, enough interesting plot twists to keep the viewer engaged, and some songs to divert everyone. All the critics mentioned Mae West's rendition of "Frankie and Johnny," a ballad about ill-fated lovers that usually was performed as a torch song; when sung by West, it became a mocking and assertive comment on romance. Her unique style was perfect for Diamond Lil. West loved the elaborate turn-of-the-century gowns that suited her figure and the jewelry she considered essential for a successful woman; and, of course, she loved being surrounded by admiring men.

West used the tightly corseted, floor-length dresses of the 1890s to full advantage. She was the sexiest woman around, she asserted as she slowly sashayed across the stage in a long dress that revealed a generous bosom. To the 1920s women in the audience, dressed in the loose-fitting short dresses that were stylish then, the thought that 1890s dresses were sexy was laughable. Further, West, not a conventional beauty, kept reminding everyone (as did all of the men in the play) that she was the most desirable, attractive woman in the world; these words evoked peals of laughter. Was she kidding? Did she take herself seriously? No one could be sure.

With the successful launching of *Diamond Lil,* West began a practice that continued for the rest of her life: she created her own version of her past for the play's program and for all interviewers. In 1929, for example, when she appeared in *Diamond Lil* in Chicago, the program notes listed her age as "barely twenty-seven years old," when in fact she was going on thirty-six. The program notes also told readers that she lived in Kew Gardens, Long Island, with her mother and sister and gave the impression of a vital but demure young woman, quite a different image from Diamond Lil. She sometimes described her mother, who was from Bavaria, as a French model, and never mentioned her brief marriage to Frank Wallace. West always claimed to be married to her fans and to her career.

In a souvenir program for *Diamond Lil,* Mae West described the title character and the general plot line of the play. She asked rhetorically: "Could Diamond Lil love any one more than herself. . . . Love anything better than the white flame of her diamonds or the red flame of men's passions?" The answer was clear to all who knew the Lil/Mae character. Although she acknowledged that Lil was a harlot, she added: "Men had to pay heavy, if they wanted her—and it is true that she did want to be paid. Still, she was not an ordinary trollop. She had brains where they belong. . . ordinary bawds had their brains where. . . . " She did not have to finish the sentence. In 1928, this was considered heady stuff. The decade may have been roaring and bootleggers may have been enjoying their profits, but rarely did the underworld appear on Broadway having so much fun. The good succeed and the bad are punished; that was the moral principle by which most mainstream entertainment lived. Mae West challenged this guideline and her sold-out audiences every night shared in her joke.

Mae West's message in *Diamond Lil* was, indeed, subversive. She departed from the usual stereotypical treatment of prostitutes by making Diamond Lil independent, successful, and dominant; she was not a victim who was used and misused by men, and whose fate was determined by circumstances beyond her control. West's Lil used men, and she was always in control. Because she was placed in the 1890s, removed from the so-called liberated 1920s, the audience could enjoy the portrayal without feeling threatened by it. Both men and women could view Lil as an atypical, humorous rendition of an old stereotype. And since Mae West considered herself an original, everyone was happy.

Mae West wrote two more plays before moving on to Hollywood. The first, *Pleasure Man,* opened at the Biltmore in New York on October 1, 1928, and lasted only two performances. West was still performing in *Diamond Lil* at the time and claimed to have written it while doing *Lil. Pleasure Man* revealed her continued interest in describing the behind-the-scenes lives of female impersonators; it also featured thwarted lovers, murder, and castration. West did not appear in it. The plot was confusing, and the lurid third-act castration scene assured the show's closing. Many of the reviews were of the preview performances at the Bronx Opera House in September 1928. Jack Conway of *Variety* said, "It's the queerest show you've ever seen. All of the Queens are in it." He went on to describe the controversial scene where a man murdered his wife's seducer. "It seems he was a medical student and he explained he didn't intend to kill him, just wanted to fix it so he wouldn't do any more stepping, and performed an operation. Can you imagine!"

It was no surprise that the show did not last on Broadway. West challenged the censors who had forced the show's closing. She took the case to court, insisting that *Pleasure Man* was not an immoral play. This time she eventually won in court, but by then, 1930, she had moved on to other projects. The publicity associated with *Pleasure Man* surely helped the box-office receipts of *Diamond Lil,* which was playing only a few blocks away.

The next play, *The Constant Sinner,* was based on a novel called *Babe Gordon* that West wrote while on tour with *Diamond Lil.* The novel became a best seller; the play opened at the Royale Theater on September 14, 1931, where it played for sixty-four performances. West starred as Babe, an immoral woman. The shocking aspect of this play, however, was not the West character, but rather the interracial love theme. Although the leading man was played by a white actor in black makeup, the subject scandalized audiences.

In a preview performance in Atlantic City, *The Constant Sinner* drew a standing-room-only crowd. The *Atlantic City Press* found it entertaining. "Miss West handles her role with surety and a sufficiency of wise-cracks that provides laughter with frequency." The lurid story line, with Babe Gordon consorting with Money Johnson, the "colored king of Harlem's dope ring," titillated audiences. When the play opened on Broadway in September 1931, the *New York Times* reviewer panned it. He deplored Mae West's slouching around the stage, " . . . her vocal stunts, her exploitation of blonde buxomness—all these grow pretty tiresome through repetition." He concluded his review: "Seldom, come to think of it, has fouler talk been heard on the Broadway stage, even in these frank and forward times."

Mae West's interest, indeed eagerness, to explore the underworld, something rarely seen on mainstream stages, shocked the critics and began to drive audiences away. Her fondness for gangsters, dope dealers, shady ladies, and honky-tonk environments was not shared by most middle-class Americans. Working-class men and college boys had always been the backbone of her constituency, but there were not enough of them to keep *The Constant Sinner* before the public. Further, the unceasing publicity, even though West viewed all publicity as good, did not attract audiences this time. The interracial theme undoubtedly contributed to the difficulty. Audiences in the 1930s might have accepted whores with good hearts, but not white whores with black lovers. The inclusion of dope dealing only accentuated the depravity that many now assumed was standard fare for a Mae West play.

Robert Benchley, the witty writer for the urbane *New Yorker* magazine, proclaimed in 1930 (quite possibly with West in mind) that he, for one, felt

> that sex, as a theatrical property, is tiresome as the Old Mortgage, and that I don't want to hear it mentioned ever again. I am sick of rebellious youth and I am sick of Victorian parents and I don't care if all the little girls in all sections of the United States get ruined or want to get ruined or keep from getting ruined. All I ask is: don't write plays about it and ask me to sit through them.

Mae West obliged Mr. Benchley. *The Constant Sinner* was her last Broadway offering.

With the exception of *Diamond Lil,* where the sexual content was mixed with humor, and good-time gal Lil's dubious activities were safely in her past, Mae West's sexual plays scandalized Broadway but did not become box-office successes. *Sex,* the first of the sequence, caused a sensation because it was new and audacious; her subsequent entries, *The Drag, The Constant Sinner,* and *Pleasure Man,* were too raw, especially for middle-class women.

West had now written six plays in as many years. They explored illicit sex, homosexuality, infidelity, interracial love affairs, castration, violence, and corruption, as well as other aspects of the seamier sides of life. They brought into respectable Broadway theaters scenes in seafront cafes, Harlem dives, saloons, and dope-dealing brothels. Thanks to newspaper coverage, middle- and upper-class American women could read about these lurid subjects while drinking their morning coffee. They had seen Mae West's picture in newspapers and magazines and knew she was more daring than most bawdy women entertainers because she was willing to discuss forbidden subjects in theatrical form, not just in the naughty songs sung on vaudeville stages and in night clubs. Hypocrisy and double standards were accepted features of respectable life; indeed, some argued that the only way to ensure civil relations between the sexes was to allow the wilder dimensions of male society to exist, albeit in dark places with no respectable person speaking for them or of them.

Mae West's plays rejected this rationale. She knew too many bankers and businessmen who frequented brothels and dope dens to think that the appearance of propriety ensured respectability. Rather, such men protected their pleasure and their family life by living double lives and moralizing against the secret illicit lives they led. For it was often these very same men who spoke out against immorality on Broadway stages. Mae West's sheer honesty kept her from tolerating this hypocritical posture. Further, she believed that sexual activity was healthy and natural, that women had as much right to sexual pleasure as men, and that all forms of sexual behavior should be given a respectable hearing. Of course, she also believed in exploiting topics that would fill the theaters in which she performed.

None of Mae West's plays were preachy. There were no long speeches summarizing her point of view. Rather, her female characters became symbols of her point of view. Margie La-

Mont, Diamond Lil, and Babe Gordon were good-time women who knew how to pursue their goals and how to give up when they lost. They made fun of all forms of pomposity and were themselves the butt of the joke on occasion. None of the plays could be labeled riveting theater; as numerous critics noted, the dialogue was often stilted and the performers wooden.

Although West liked to be surrounded by male admirers on stage, occasionally she was willing to have a single man around who played hard to get; it added to the excitement and mystery of the story. She was even willing to give up a guy she liked because she knew there would be another one soon enough. All of these features of a Mae West story would be displayed, even more favorably, in the movies. But in the permissive 1920s, West's plays were at the very radical end of the wide spectrum of Broadway entertainment. None of the plays, with the possible exception of *Diamond Lil,* withstands the test of time.

By 1931, Mae West had polished her public image to perfection. She was a force, a personality who took charge of any and all situations, an initiator who shaped her own destiny. Her every action enforced this view. The name Mae West evoked a clear picture: a funny, seductive woman who loved to talk about sex and to practice it as often as possible. No one was lukewarm toward her; you either liked her or you did not. Few other public personalities at that time commanded a similar name recognition. She benefited from the negative publicity accompanying her allegedly scandalous plays and confirmed most of America's opinion that New York City was the center of sin and corruption. To her credit, she converted this seemingly negative view to a positive one, ensuring her even greater visibility in the unlikely venue of the movies.

Mae West's Broadway years were brief. They coincided with a period of amazing variety and vitality on New York's stages, and they gave Mae West the opportunity to distinguish herself from the other bawdy practitioners. Her wisecracking personality seemed to be better suited than the rest to constant media coverage, and her obvious enjoyment of her star status came through to her many fans. West benefited from the spread of New York culture to every corner of America. Although she was a quintessential New Yorker, her image and message traveled effectively across the country to big and small cities.

CHAPTER THREE

Goodness Had Nothing to Do with It

1933–1943

The Great Depression that began in 1929 devastated Broadway theater. In 1931–1932, of the 152 plays performing that season, 121 closed quickly. Show business, like every other business, was adversely affected by the downturn in the economy. As much as Americans wished to be amused and were willing to pay for entertainment, unemployed people could not afford even the lowered ticket prices for a play. Although the situation would improve later in the decade, things looked bleak for Broadway in 1930. The radio, silent films, and the new sound films offered cheaper opportunities for diversion. Eva Tanguay had retired from vaudeville by this time; Sophie Tucker was continuing to perform in night clubs, but for less money; Moms Mabley appeared in black musical shows, and Fanny Brice tried movies but gave them up in favor of the other new mass medium, radio.

Mae West, ever interested in pursuing her career in new settings, looked to Hollywood, California. During the heyday of the silent era, moviemakers had relied on home-grown talent or on people without theatrical experience. After all, you did not have to learn lines in silent film. If you could take direction, you could be an actor, or so thought the film producers. But many of these actors could not make the transition to sound movies.

Their voices and their mannerisms were unsuited to the new medium. So Hollywood looked to the Broadway theater for new faces and talent. The Twentieth Century Limited, the luxurious coast-to-coast railroad car, began transporting actresses to Hollywood and back to New York throughout the 1930s. Many stars alternated between a Broadway play and a movie, six months in one location, six months in the other. Katharine Hepburn, who came to Hollywood around the same time as Mae West, did just that. Mae West, by contrast, stayed in movies for the next decade.

Sound movies turned out to be a successful phenomenon. After weathering a poor economy and a rocky transition from silent to sound, the good times returned by 1933 and Hollywood prospered. Movie producers, hungry for new stories and new stars, used Broadway plays and best-selling novels as the basis for their new movies. The plots, whether they were melodramas, comedies, adventures, or musicals, were transferred, often by the same writers, from play or novel to movie script. Audiences' familiarity with the material and the stars was an added attraction.

Talking pictures had begun modestly with a sound portion in *The Jazz Singer* in 1927. Hollywood studios, beginning with Warner Brothers, made the risky and expensive transition to new equipment and new methods to accommodate sound. By the end of 1930, more than 13,000 theaters around the country were equipped for sound. This left about 8,000 theaters, located mostly in rural areas, that still showed only silent films; they lingered into the 1930s and then died.

New stars had to be acquired whose voices were suitable for "talkies." Everyone was pleasantly surprised in 1931 when the Swedish beauty, Greta Garbo, made her first sound movie, *Anna Christie*. The ads read, "Garbo Talks!" Audiences discovered that her low, slightly accented English was easily understood and did not put off the fans. Mae West's thick Brooklyn accent, her nasal intonation, and her somewhat thin voice did not seem well suited to sound movies, but her success surprised her producers.

The movies turned out to be an even more demanding mistress than Broadway and vaudeville. The audiences were insatiable; new stars and new stories were in constant demand. The competition was keen, a situation well known to Mae West. Approached in the 1920s about the possibility of doing a movie, she had been reluctant to leave the Broadway stage. But the time was now propitious, and she was nothing if not ambitious and eager to conquer another province. As she told the reporters at the time: "I'm not a little girl from a little town here to make good in a big town. I'm a big girl from a big town who's come to make good in a little town." The Mae West ego was firmly intact. She was in Hollywood looking for new admirers, new frontiers, and new excitements.

Sound film, which allowed West's witty repartée to be heard, was better suited to her talents than silent films. Surely her facial expressions and slow, swinging walk could have been effective in silent film, but the intimacy of her voice and its intonations, pauses, and rhythms could only be captured in sound film. Indeed, women comics, who had been second bananas in silent film, flourished in sound. Silent comedy had been an almost exclusively male preserve dominated by the physical antics of Charlie Chaplin, Harold Lloyd, and Buster Keaton. But once the talkies came, women could be accepted as funny people. They could whip off a quick one-liner or caustic retort as well as a man. Slapstick comedy remained on the sound screen, but it now had an effective companion, verbal comedy. And Mae West was to become the queen of witticisms, quick retorts, and immensely quotable one-liners (all of the chapter titles in this book, of course, are Westisms).

None of West's appeal was evident in January 1932 when she arrived in Hollywood. It was unknown whether her persona would translate successfully to film and command the large, diverse audience that Hollywood required. She was thirty-eight years old; by all accounts, in good health and good shape, but still a well-known commodity whose appeal seemed limited to the boisterous audience that had first met her in vaudeville. Further, film was a very different enterprise from vaudeville or the

Broadway stage. West was used to controlling every production she was in; in Hollywood, there were producers, directors, writers, set designers, costumers, and a whole host of technical staff who collaborated on a movie production. Each took pride in his or her contribution and each took some credit for the success of the outcome. No one volunteered to accept the blame for a failure, however.

Mae West herself was not sure about this new medium. As she noted in her autobiography: "Could I show my stuff in the city of oranges, Warner Brothers and swimming pools? I had no doubt about my talents, but I was aware I faced a barrier." She knew that the movies had wide distribution and could make a national star out of an unknown or a local star. West was an established performer in New York and New Haven, but how would her bald discussions of sex be received in small-town America? Was she an easterner who could not adapt to the Land of Sunshine? In New York, she and Timony arranged the financing for all of her plays and enjoyed good returns on their investment. In Hollywood she no longer controlled the finances; Hollywood movies were financed by New York bankers who did not rely solely on personal familiarity in making deals. They also were very cautious when hundreds of thousands of dollars were at stake.

West rarely discussed her competition. She never deigned to acknowledge that there were other stars who challenged her status as the sex goddess of America. Marlene Dietrich and Greta Garbo, two foreign actresses, were already household names by the early 1930s. Clara Bow, the "It" girl, had been Paramount Studios' biggest silent screen sexpot. Mae West, when asked by interviewers what she thought of this star or that star, always replied that she did not know her work and doubted that anyone duplicated her (West's) personality. She usually said it with a sly smile on her face, thereby avoiding the accusation of being arrogant.

Mae West planned to carve out a special niche for herself: that of a sex comedienne. She was not to be a tragic romantic sex goddess, like Garbo or resigned and jaded, like Dietrich.

She was to wisecrack about a subject that others took seriously. Further, because her audience assumed she was joking when she described herself as the sexiest woman alive, they laughed at her constant discussions of sex. Audiences, by contrast, cried when Garbo died for love or shook their heads grimly when Marlene Dietrich destroyed a man for love. Jean Harlow, who was also a sex comedienne, was much more attractive than West, so when she combined humor with a healthy attitude toward sex, people laughed in admiration. With West, they laughed in disbelief.

Wisecracking, of course, was not unique to Mae West. Eve Arden and Lucille Ball played wisecracking second bananas to female leads in movies throughout the 1930s. Both women could be relied on to provide the heroine with comic relief as well as emotional support. Carole Lombard played a dizzy blonde who uttered clever lines as if by accident, and Myrna Loy exchanged sophisticated banter with her movie husband, William Powell, in their very successful series of *Thin Man* films. But no one compared with Mae West as a central character, a star whose primary asset was her wry, sly, clever remarks about sex.

In the early 1930s, there were a number of big studios vying for stars and screenplays. They each marked out a different turf in order to gain distinctiveness. Metro-Goldwyn-Mayer (MGM), for example, one of the most prestigious studios, claimed to have the greatest romantic heroes and heroines, such as Clark Gable, Robert Taylor, Greta Garbo, and Joan Crawford, and to make the greatest melodramas, romances, and historical films in the world. Warner Brothers, on the other hand, had James Cagney, Humphrey Bogart, and Bette Davis in its pantheon and concentrated on thrillers and stories of big-city crime and urban violence. Paramount Studios, where Mae West went, was known as the home of sophisticated foreigners, with Marlene Dietrich among its stars and Ernst Lubitsch among its great directors. Paramount was run by Adolph Zukor and Jesse Lasky.

Although the studio heads had a great deal of influence over which movies were made and how much the stars were paid, the studio's producers were responsible for the development of the films; that is, it was their task to bring together a workable script, a star, a supporting cast, and all of the technical crew necessary to make a movie. Two producers at Paramount, William LeBaron, who had known West in New York, and Emanuel Z. Cohen, were instrumental in bringing Mae West to the studio and keeping her happy, a mighty undertaking. Initially, she had to learn the trade, the ins and outs of the town and its politics, and which were the trump cards that would allow her to get her way. The girl from Brooklyn had to be convinced that sunny California was conducive to her brand of humor, and she had to demonstrate her popularity to more skeptical producers.

West rented a flat at the Ravenswood, an apartment hotel on Rossmore Avenue in Hollywood. Little did she know that this supposedly temporary apartment would remain her principal residence for the rest of her life. She went on Paramount Studios' payroll while they prepared a script in which she was to have a significant role. The movie was *Night After Night* and was billed as a starring vehicle for a new male talent, George Raft. While West waited for the script to be ready, the studio paid her $5,000 a week. Both the sum and the experience were unprecedented for Mae West. She was not used to taking money for waiting, nor was she used to being a pawn in someone else's game. She was a doer, a controller of her own productions and her own destiny. Paramount assured her that this was the way things worked in Hollywood. She was not at all sure that its way and hers were compatible.

When Mae West read the completed script for *Night After Night,* her worst fears were realized. She found the part written for her to be unacceptable and she refused to do it. The producers were frantic. Al Kaufman, one of the executives, invited West and Jim Timony out to dinner. Before the conversation began, West opened her purse and gave Kaufman a check for $20,000. He asked what it was for. West told him that it was for the four weeks she had been sitting around Hollywood and that she was going back to New York the next day. Kaufman, thinking fast, asked her to consider this deal: she could rewrite her part and bring it to the studio the next afternoon; then the cast and crew would rehearse the original script, followed by her version. Whichever was better would stay, and if she did not agree with the decision, she could leave.

According to Hollywood legend, Mae West accepted the challenge. As Adolph Zukor summed up the result in his autobiography: "Plainly her own characterization was far better. The public thought Mae knew what she was about too, for in *Night After Night* she stole the show." George Raft later said that West stole everything but the camera. Her part was small but memorable. It was in her first scene that she got off one of her most famous one-liners. West entered a night club and the hat-check girl said: "My goodness, what beautiful diamonds." West answered: "Goodness had nothing to do with it." After delivering that line, West slowly sashayed up the stairs. The film's director, Archie Mayo, wanted to cut the scene right after her line, whereas West wanted the camera to follow her slow, swaying ascent. They filmed it both ways, but the final version was Mayo's. Audiences were expected to get the point without Mae West's elaborate visual explanation. West was learning about the value of timing as an important film technique; although she lost some battles over how scenes were shot, she won the war. *Night After Night* was a Prohibition romance with Mae West providing the comic relief. Most critics singled out her performance for special praise. Paramount quickly searched for the next vehicle to display her talents.

Perhaps, Mae West thought, Hollywood was not as bad as she feared. The money was good and future opportunities might fulfill her hopes. Paramount owned 1,700 theaters around the country and more people than she could ever play before in the theater would witness her talents on the screen. It seemed quite possible that she could win national popularity. She was associated with a powerful studio that had formidable publicity machinery. Further, Paramount's ability to place its films in its own theaters assured any new star of immediate exposure to multitudes of people.

Paramount Studios turned out to be a good choice for Mae West. After Warner Brothers, Paramount made the most movies of any studio. In the year West traveled to Hollywood, Paramount produced fifty-one movies, 10 percent of all the movies made that year (Warner's made fifty-three). If West proved popular, Paramount would contract her to do multiple films a year. Her flamboyant style harmonized with Paramount's aggressive approach to marketing. West began a practice with her next film, *She Done Him Wrong,* that she was to follow throughout her film career: she made personal appearances in big cities when her movie opened. It was vaudeville all over again. At the Paramount Theater in New York, her fans could be relied on to come out for every new Mae West film. The trouper in Mae, the lover of a live audience, was able to rekindle that experience while promoting her latest Paramount release. Audiences flocked to see Mae West both in person and on celluloid. She would often sing a few songs from the movie before it played. Her supreme self-confidence in her ability to entertain an audience was confirmed.

The personal appearances that accompanied her movie releases throughout the 1930s demonstrated her love of live performing and her unwillingness to lose direct touch with her fans. West's devotion to her followers was a constant theme in her many interviews with the press. She always presented herself as a follower of her fans' wishes. That is why, she said, she had never married—her fans required her full-time attention. Clearly, the positive reinforcement she derived from performing, the enthusiastic applause she received, energized her. Paradoxically, although movies, unlike vaudeville, supposedly did not require constant travel, Mae West traveled extensively to promote each new movie. The often arduous schedules, long train rides, dirt, and dust never seemed to discourage or tire her. Mae West's many years on the stage had convinced her that live appearances confirmed her worth. They became the measure of her success. Box-office receipts would impress Hollywood, but-the trouper in Mae always wanted to hear the applause for her-self; her need for it seemed insatiable.

In 1933, when she brought her play *Diamond Lil* to the screen under the title *She Done Him Wrong,* Mae West was forty years old and going strong. What was truly amazing was that the public image she projected was only slightly different from the 1928 Di-amond Lil theatrical personality, or the 1920 night club singer of "Frankie and Johnny," or, still earlier, the shimmy dancer in vaudeville. The number of one-liners, of course, had increased, and the shocking settings of her Broadway plays had disap-peared. The story lines of her films were tamer and better thought-out than her plays, although none of Mae West's films could be accused of having substantial plots. The question was whether West's clearly defined image as a mocker of sexual mo-res in America could appeal to a large and diverse audience. She had her following on Broadway and the vaudeville circuit but movies, a mass medium, required the ability to attract large au-diences in both small-town and urban America, in both immi-grant and native neighborhoods. Would her appeal be broad enough to make her movies successful?

Mae West's vaudeville background was quite apparent in her Hollywood movies: she sang in most of them, sometimes danced, and was always surrounded by large casts, usually con-sisting of adoring males. Spectacle followed by unrelated scenes, something vaudeville audiences were accustomed to, often char-acterized her movies. This often confused and exasperated the big-city film critics, but, to the studio's relief, it did not perturb the audiences. They just kept coming. Zukor and his colleagues took credit for understanding West's appeal. The other studios clearly were wrong in thinking that her "lusty sex," as Zukor called it, could not be translated to the screen. It could, and Par-amount's risk paid off. Most of West's films, especially her early ones, were enormously profitable.

William LeBaron, her producer, and Zukor, her boss, cred-ited Mae West with helping the studio to overcome its financial problems. Paramount had gone into receivership in January 1933, primarily because it had overextended itself by a massive-buying campaign of new theaters at a time when business was declining; within two years, the studio had been successfully reorganized and the rumored threat of an MGM takeover passed. Mae West's films may not have been the only factor in turning the studio around, but they surely contributed a great deal. The negative print of *She Done Him Wrong,* for example, cost $200,000, but the film's domestic gross was more than $2 million—the film earned ten times its cost, not including foreign distribution receipts. Mae West's brand of humor traveled quite well, to the tune of an additional $1 million in revenue per film.

Bad economic times, ironically, are good times for show business. People need relief from the anxiety of joblessness, the fear of losing a job, and the uncertainty of future possibilities. Theater owners sometimes had to lower the ticket price in order to attract the audience, but film audiences increased in size. In the mid-1930s, for example, 60 million people went to the movies each week, half of the nation's population. Movies became, after radio, a national cultural experience. No matter where you lived, small town, farm, or big city, East, West, North, or South, you could attend the latest Mae West movie, the latest adventure, and the newest Marx Brothers comedy. Movies united Americans and gave them heroes and heroines to share, common dreams, and a shared vocabulary of concerns. Movie magazines and newspaper reviews acquainted people with the stars' biographies as well as the plots of the movies.

Movies provided pleasant fantasies as well as adventures. Movie viewers traveled all over the globe, saw splendid costumes, and experienced excitement and vicarious drama. There is no evidence that movie fans who were themselves experiencing hard times resented movies about the rich and powerful. Although critics claimed that the very escapism of such films prevented viewers from living their lives realistically, fans blithely kept going to the movies. One high school senior in

Denver captured many peoples' feelings about the movies in a letter that appeared in the February 1933 issue of *The New Movie Magazine:* "The movies mean much to me as a broadening and cultural agent in my life, and I am for them."

Movies stars entered the mental universes of all moviegoers. Stars encouraged and extended their influence over their fans by endorsing products, appearing on radio shows, and making personal appearances throughout the country. The importance of stars and the number of fans expanded dramatically during the depression years of the 1930s, phenomena that are well known in recent times. However, the blossoming of popular cultural forms, particularly movies, was a new spectacle in the 1930s. The quantity of movies produced increased and the moviegoing audiences got their ten or twelve cents' worth of entertainment: a newsreel, an episode in an adventure serial, and a double feature of films. An evening or afternoon at the movies lasted three and a half to four hours.

The profit margin was impressive, and bankers in New York became more willing to finance Hollywood productions. Foreign talent poured into the United States. With the Nazis in Germany determining film policy and the rest of Europe in an economic depression, writers, directors, actors, cinematographers, and producers came to Hollywood, where conversations in German, French, Italian, and Russian could be heard at the many parties held in the sumptuous mansions of the film community. The myth and mystique of Hollywood also developed and flourished during this period, awakening the hopes of many aspiring actors from around the country. Photographs of palm trees, luxurious salmon-colored Spanish-style homes, and glamorous stars appeared in the many different movie magazines created to service this new phenomenon: the fan. The public's interest in reading about the stars seemed unending.

Mae West had to become accustomed to the process of moviemaking; she found, fortunately, that the producers and crew were willing to cooperate with her once they determined that she was a box-office success. Then West could operate as she pleased; she rewrote scripts, insisted upon credit for the screenplay and the original dialogue, and was paid for writing in addition to her acting fee. Mae West and her manager-agent, Jim Timony, turned out to be good businesspeople. They invested West's huge salary wisely in real estate in the San Fernando Valley, a relatively undeveloped area north of Los Angeles, and on the beach front in Malibu. She also maintained her apartment in Hollywood, where she stayed during the work week.

West had a great deal of influence in picking the cast for her movies. Legend has it that she saw the very young Cary Grant on the lot at Paramount and suggested him to play opposite her in *She Done Him Wrong*. He also appeared in her next movie, *I'm No Angel*. After that, Grant's star soared and he was unavailable for future Mae West movies. In fact, West only surrounded herself with less well-known (and often less talented) stars. In one area, however, West showed her generosity: she hired black actresses and black male musicians in many of her movies. While Duke Ellington led his band in one West movie, black actresses like Louise Beavers played her maid; true, the black maid role was a stereotype, but in a period when few black actors were employd in the movies, it was a step forward.

Making a high-budget movie in Hollywood during the early 1930s usually took fifteen to twenty weeks. Mae West assured her producers at Paramount that her Diamond Lil story could be filmed in much less time. Although they were skeptical, they met her request to allow a week of rehearsals prior to filming, an unusual action; much to their surprise, the movie was made in eighteen days. West's Broadway experience stood her in good stead in Hollywood. She knew how to memorize lines and long scenes, something many Hollywood actors could not do. Those who had started in silent films were used to the director talking them through a scene; they had no lines to memorize and hardly had to know the story line in advance. But West had to acclimate herself to working before a camera rather than a live audience, a difficult task for a comic. She could not measure the success of a line or a gesture without human reaction, but being the veteran she was, West already knew where the laughs came and how to exploit those moments.

Paramount broke an understanding and a precedent by producing *Diamond Lil*. The play had been banned by Hollywood's self-censorship organization, the Hays Office, and when rumors started that the studio was turning it into a movie, Will Hays, the head of the censorship group, and his West Coast colleagues wrote urgent memos advising the studio to cease and desist. Hollywood had been regulating itself since 1922, when the Motion Picture Producers and Directors Association had hired Hays to oversee the industry. However, Hays had acted more as a public relations advocate for the movies than as a censor. That changed in 1934. Pressure had been mounting for the industry to regulate itself. A Production Code was developed by the studios, which required all scripts and all final cuts of the films to be approved before release by the censorship office they supported. Though West claimed that she learned how to get around the Production Code, as it came to be called, it surely reined her in. Frequently, she later recounted, she threw in some purposely crude lines only to have the censors cut them out, thereby satisfying them while it did no harm to the script. West claimed that "religious groups and some lunatic fringe women's organizations" wished her restrained, but that the popularity of her movies confirmed her wide appeal to the general public. "Every person who is not a moron or a mental defective of some sort carries a very effective censor and super-critic of his actions in his cerebral cortex and in his heart. If that doesn't work, no amount of censorship from the outside will do anybody any good. None of this," she assured her readers, "affected my personal life."

Joseph I. Breen, who headed the Hollywood office of the censors, believed that Mae West required a team of diligent censors to control her. In one memo to his staff, he noted:

Difficulty is inherent with a Mae West picture. Lines and pieces of business, which in the script seem to be thoroughly innocuous, turn out when shown on the screen to be questionable at best, when they are not definitely offensive. A special memorandum should be prepared on this matter for presentation to Mr. Hays.

A wink of the eye, a flick of a fan, and a carefully orchestrated walk up a staircase were all West trademarks that exasperated the moral censors. Besides the spice, audiences probably enjoyed the suspense, wondering with each new Mae West movie what ways she had devised to fool the censors.

The excitement and uncertainty that surrounded every movie battle between Mae West and the censors could not be avoided. Her subject matter, her manner, and her settings were in direct opposition to the Production Code. According to a handbook written by Breen's secretary on the meanings of the code: "A story may be entirely moral in its theme and thesis, but its moral effect on the audience would be entirely nullified if many of the scenes were to be played in dives, saloons, and bedrooms." This stricture in effect eliminated Mae West's favorite settings for her movies. The handbook, which instructed the studios, further elaborates: " . . . and if the players' gestures and postures were suggestive and offensive; and, further, if the story were replete with vulgar, double-meaning dialogue . . . " the material would be objectionable. Without double meanings, a Mae West film would lose its essence. The two, Mae West and the Production Code, were inherently incompatible. As a result, all of West's movies were subject to stringent examination with scenes cut, changed, or deleted to accommodate the regulators.

Paramount ignored the voluntary strictures of the 1933 Hays Office only to face the more demanding guidelines after the code was instituted in 1934. Indeed, the whole industry suffered from the restrictions placed upon it. Mae West, surely, was not solely to blame for the 1934 Production Code, but she contributed more than her fair share to its implementation. *She Done Him Wrong,* the 1933 movie version of *Diamond Lil,* had the same basic story of a former prostitute, now named Lady Lou, who was the mistress of a saloon owner named Gus Jordan. Still set in the Gay Nineties, the movie opened with Lady Lou, holding forth in the back room of the saloon, exchanging wisecracks with the admiring men and singing many of her favorite songs. Prostitution, gambling, dope dealing, and sundry other vices were presented as harmless, exaggerated activities engaged in by colorful people, rather than as dangerous and immoral.

The story's adventure was provided by an undercover police agent, played by Cary Grant in his first major role, masquerading as a Salvation Army missionary. The romantic interest was heightened because Grant played hard to get and West had to work hard to win him. In an early scene that would become famous, she stood at the top of the staircase of the saloon, looked down at the handsome missionary, leered, and said: "Come up and see me some time. You can be had." Adolph Zukor later said that the line "became as much a part of the depression era as the Sheik and 'It' had been of the early and later twenties." He added: "When you speak of eras, I'd say Mae was in command during the depression years. Mae surprised us, and maybe herself. But Mae knew her talents in relation to the audiences—which is always what counts—better than we did."

Besides the famous staircase line, delivered while swaggering around the saloon, West threw off other one-liners, the first batch in a long series that would become associated with her name and would be collected in book form in the 1960s. "When a woman goes wrong, a man goes right after her," she noted in this film. Another notable exchange was with Cary Grant, who asked her: "Haven't you ever met a man who could make you happy?" West answered: "Sure. Lots of times." At the end of the movie, when Grant arrested her along with the other bad guys, he first slipped a diamond ring on her finger, assuring the audience that romance would win in the end. He said: "You bad girl." And she replied: "You'll find out." Fade out.

Audiences loved the naughty Mae who seemed always interested in either talking about sex or engaging in it. West reinforced this image in the many interviews she granted. She told reporter Gladys Hall (*Movie Classic,* August 1933) that: "I can take 'em or leave 'em. I'm just like a man with my romances—here today and gone tomorrow.... Men are conveniences to me, nothing more." Her quick witticisms became good copy for eager reporters. She told fans in the December 1933 issue of *Screen Play* what sex appeal was: "It is the radiation of an attractive personality and demands intelligence, first of all." When asked who thought up the line "Come up and see me some time," she answered: "Probably Delilah. I will only take the credit for reviving it for screen purposes."

In answer to a fan's question as to why her movies always were about sex, she replied that sex is what kept the world revolving. "If the public did not like sex pictures," she continued, "yours truly wouldn't play in them.... After all, sex is life, creation, and no creative art can dodge the vital issue of sex." She concluded the interview by saying that her writing and acting were the most important things in her life. Although she liked children, she was not married and therefore said she could not discuss that subject. A practical and knowing Mae West, indeed almost at times a prim-sounding West, combined propriety and boldness, a rebel and a conventional woman, all wrapped up in one dynamic package.

Surely she laughed when she read an item in the August, 1934 issue of *Photoplay* that described a school child in Waldo, Kansas, who signed his math paper "Mae West." When asked for an explanation by the teacher, the child said that he had signed her name "Because I done 'em wrong." Her one-liners and her image had conquered the country. West noted in an interview in *Modern Screen* in July 1933 that it was getting hard for her to preserve her originality, as imitators quickly cropped up. Her wiggle, she said, was copied by the kids at Hollywood High School and after she painted her nails with a platinum polish, "...the next day everybody but Mae had platinum nails. So Mae gives up."

The songs Mae West sang in *She Done Him Wrong* contributed to the bawdy image. "A Guy What Takes His Time" and "I Wonder Where My Easy Rider's Gone" were unsubtle descriptions of love-making. West's nasal soprano punctuated the lyrics with cries of "oh, oh, oh." The words of "A Guy What Takes His Time" include "A hurry-up affair, I always give the air," and "There is no fun in getting something done when you are rushed. . . ." "Easy Rider," a slang term for pimp, included West moaning and wondering when her easy rider would return. She also sang "Frankie and Johnny," the traditional love song about a woman whose lover cheated on her and whom she shoots in anger, despair, and pain. Lady Lou sang the song ironically, as she would never allow any man to win her affections and thereby make her vulnerable to his rejection.

Mae West's renditions of these songs fit into the bawdy blues singer tradition of Bessie Smith, Sophie Tucker, and Fanny Brice. Brice's "I'd Rather Be Blue Over You Than Happy With Someone Else" made the message clear, Tucker reminded her lovers that "Mamma Goes Where Pappa Goes," and Bessie Smith sang the very explicit "Copulating Blues." The big difference between the bawdy singers' style and Mae West's was her mocking tone and her obvious command of the situation. The other bawdy singers acknowledged their loves and their interest in sex, but, unlike West they depended upon the men to satisfy them and to be true to them. West reversed the roles. As she told the movie magazine interviewers, she took men that interested her, enjoyed them, and then moved on to the next conquest. She did not invest romantically or psychologically in them. She left them, she done them wrong; they never had the chance to do her wrong.

The movie critics generally liked *She Done Him Wrong*. *Variety* credited director Lowell Sherman with restraining Mae, "something Mae has never been able to do on her own." And the *New York Times* film critic grudgingly acknowledged that "with the haughty strut and the nasal twang which are the principal assets of her repertoire, she filled the screen with gaudy humor." Movie audiences, they admitted, were now able to see what New York had been admiring for a decade. Mae West found adoring audiences in Chicago, Los Angeles, and all of the cities in between. She enjoyed the touring, especially to the cities where she had played in vaudeville. It was like going home again. She was able to recreate the experience while viewing herself on celluloid. She could now be assured that her inimitable image would be preserved forever.

She Done Him Wrong's success in the big cities was no surprise, but its popularity in small-town America delighted the cynical New York studio bankers. In cities as different as Birmingham, Alabama, and Lincoln, Nebraska, the movie played to sell-out crowds. In a period when movies usually played for a one-week run, West's was held over for three weeks and often returned for additional weeks. The movie grosses and attendance records topped those of any movie since the silent film classic *Birth of a Nation*. Mae West's Brooklyn accent, her obvious gestures, and her garish style traveled better than anyone had anticipated.

Paramount Studios was thrilled. Arthur Mayer, the publicity director, later recalled the advertising campaign he devised for Mae West.

> There was no doubt that her pictures were going to be very sexy. I simply prepared one big still for my advertising campaign. It was just a bust. I built up the beauties with which nature had already so bountifully endowed her, and I wrote one line of what I thought was safe, chaste motion picture copy. The line was: "Hitting the high spots of lusty entertainment." Nothing happened.

The posters were sent out and only then did Adolph Zukor summon him and claim shock and surprise. Mayer remembered the following conversation with his boss:

> Mr. Mayer: I'm shocked...I thought you were such a gentleman and you used a dirty word.
> What do you mean, a dirty word?
> Lusty. What a word to use.
> Lusty, Mr. Zukor, you know, comes from the German word *lustig,* for life, energy, vigor. There is nothing dirty about the use of that word.

Look, Mr. Mayer, I don't need your Harvard education. When I look at that dame's tits, I know what lusty means.

Zukor's shock, according to Mayer, was only for public consumption. He too was overjoyed with the success of Mae West's first starring role.

Paramount's massive publicity campaigns for all of Mae West's early movies surely contributed to their success. A constant stream of press releases issued to the ever-hungry movie magazines and feature newspapers nourished the image of naughty Mae, outrageous Mae, ready-for-anything Mae. Numerous stories featured photographs that emphasized her ample bosom and congenial smirk. The deluge was especially fierce just before the opening of her latest movie. Then fans and others could be assured of a bumper crop of pictures and accompanying stories about the bombastic Mae West.

Douglas Gilbert, like many observers who wrote about Mae West throughout her long career, searched for explanations for her great success. He decided that she symbolized a revolt against the 1920s emancipated but emaciated woman: "Her well-rounded arms encircle a nation's desire for escape from a synthetic life to one of substance and color." West's Lady Lou/ Diamond Lil evoked the 1890s image of the well-endowed woman who displayed her female assets in her every move. This image, of course, fit in with West's aggressive sexuality. The slim-hipped, small-busted young woman of the 1920s deemphasized her sexuality, cutting her hair short and wearing loose-fitting clothes. Mae West's presentation evoked an earlier era, but her message was a modern one.

In *She Done Him Wrong*, "fallen women" are redeemed and virginity is no longer the essential trait for the respectable woman seeking a mate: "When a girl goes wrong, men go right after her." Again, West overturned accepted views and standard values. Not only do women have a sexual nature, she declared, but they have a right to express it, and they should not suffer any social consequences as a result. West's words may have caused moral outrage in some, and encouraged a censorship code for all Hollywood movies, but the audience received these views with seeming equanimity. Her fans kept coming back for more of the same. Indeed, the very sameness and predictability of her image kept her views before the public for multiple generations to hear.

Later in 1933, Mae West released her second major film, *I'm No Angel.* She was credited for both the screenplay and dialogue. The film cost $225,000 to produce and had a domestic gross income of $2,250,000; it also brought in $1 million from foreign sales. In its first week at the Paramount in New York, 180,000 people came to see it, a record for that theater. Most of the critics consider this movie to be her best. She played Tira, a vamp in a circus side show. West claimed that she had always been fascinated with zoos and circuses and loved the idea of a part in which she could play a lion tamer. The producer wanted to use a double in the lion-taming scene, but West insisted on doing it herself, a fact that did not go unnoticed in the press.

Cary Grant also starred in this movie. Although the story is rather simple and obvious, it allowed all of West's talents to be generously displayed. She sang a number of good songs, such as "I'm No Angel," "I Found a New Way to Go to Town," "I Want You—I Need You," and "They Call Me Sister Honky-Tonk." The scenery and costumes were spectacular, adoring men were everywhere, and, as usual, Mae West/Tira was the center of attention. The handsome hero, played by Grant, succumbed to her charms and everyone left the theater happy. The lyrics of the songs were even more explicit than those in *She Done Him Wrong.* In the title song, she sings: "Baby I can warn you/I can give you kisses until you walk on air," and she assured her listeners that she was no angel, which was hardly news to her fans. In "Sister Honky-Tonk," she tells her audience in the circus that she is free and easy and that "my life is my own."

One of her memorable one-liners is heard in this movie— when a man said: "If I could only trust you," her quick retort was: "Hundreds have." Other lines that were sent forth for all time included: "Take all you can get and give as little as possible," "Find 'em, fool 'em, and forget 'em," and "When I am good, I am very good but when I'm bad, I'm better." Thanks to her new fame, she posed for the magazine *Vanity Fair* as the Statue of Liberty. Critic George Jean Nathan commented that she looked more like the "Statue of Libido." Indeed, by early 1934, Mae West was such a sensation that intellectuals took notice. Articles that tried to describe her appeal appeared in such magazines as *The New Republic* and *The Nation*. She was no longer simply the property of her bawdy and boisterous fans. William Troy, writing in *The Nation*, said that she did a burlesque of burlesque. With two hit movies in one year, she had become a national phenomenon. Her salary from those two movies made her the eighth-highest-paid actor in Hollywood in 1933, only her second year in filmland.

West claimed in her autobiography that she never became part of the Hollywood scene because movie people were too superficial and drank too much. "So I picked my company with care, and never became part of the social life of the town—and I resented their intrusion into my love life—the stories in the magazines." She also argued that her fans, whom she cared most about, preferred that she be surrounded by mystery. Given Mae West's willingness—nay, enthusiasm—for singing and saying so much about her sexual needs, it is fascinating to note that she did not wish to share her personal life with her audience. "I kept the facts of my personal affairs, my romantic relationships strictly top secret, even keeping my public happy in the belief that I belonged entirely to them, by persistently denying for years that I had ever married." The public Mae West declared her love of love, but the private Mae West, as much as she might have been like the public West, demanded privacy.

There is another side to West's remaining apart from the Hollywood scene. Hollywood people resented the intrusion of Broadway stars, including Mae West. The incredible attention that accompanied her arrival, and especially the acclaim after *She Done Him Wrong*, was viewed coldly by Hollywood insiders.

According to columnist Ed Sullivan: "When Mae West, from Broadway, started rolling up record grosses throughout the world, the Hollywood cliques absolutely refused to attend the premiere of her pictures." The cold shoulder from the movie establishment did not seem to faze her. She created her own world, filled with admiring males who accompanied her everywhere. Jim Timony, other aides, and the latest man in her life were often photographed surrounding the smiling Mae West.

West learned quickly how to control the press treatment of her image. When printed reports circulated that she was secretly married to Jim Timony, she threatened to sue the reporter and the story was immediately retracted. She enjoyed newspaper and magazine coverage that emphasized her independence, her spunk, her talent, and her ability to overcome all odds. One compliant movie magazine reporter gushed: "All her life she's said, 'I can do it' whenever anyone scoffed 'it cannot be done.' " She fed her imaginative rendering of her personal background to reporters. To one, she maintained that her father had been a prominent featherweight boxer and that he was presently (in 1934) a chiropractor. Her sister, Beverly, told another reporter that Mae's German mother was French. Because reporters did not bother to verify any of these biographical facts, the same fabrications appeared over and over in features about her.

I'm No Angel did well all over the country. In New York, of course, it met expectations: the first week, the Paramount Theater reported grosses of $85,000, followed by $75,000 the next week. The *Variety* reporter noted that "Ushers were riding herd on a permanent corral of waitees in the lobby." In Chicago, it opened at the Oriental Theater and grossed a record $4,800 between 6 P.M. and closing time. After this success, West renegotiated her movie contract, agreeing to do two films a year for an eight-picture deal. Instead of $5,000 a week, she would receive $300,000 a picture and an extra $100,000 for the story. West was quoted as saying: "Why should I go good when I'm packin' 'em in because I'm bad?" Many of the studios scrambled to find

Mae West lookalikes. As West noted in her autobiography: "All the glamorous witchery was accompanied by bitchery, for the synthetic star often only got by for a little time before her lack of talent was detected."

Mordaunt Hall, in the *New York Times,* admitted: "She is a remarkable wit, after her fashion," and the *Variety* critic agreed that "comedy detail has been adroitly worked out and the picture is strongly fortified on laughs, all derived from the West innuendoes and the general good-natured bawdiness of the heroine, whose progress from a carnival mugg-taker to a deluxe millionaire-annexer is marked by a succession of gentlemen friends, mainly temporary and usually suckers." This last observation offered another insight into the Mae West philosophy of life: not only were men necessary to women for clearly defined purposes, but they were often gullible and easily fooled. Again, the sex-role reversal played a major role in her view of life. Whereas conventional wisdom suggested that women were ruled by their emotions and easily beguiled, West reversed that judgment, categorizing men as suckers who were easily controlled because of their active libidos.

Although there would be other hits, *She Done Him Wrong* and *I'm No Angel* received the most consistently positive reception, from both the public and the press. Further, the pattern that characterized her entire movie career was established during her first year of film making: a lot of talk about censorship and trouble with the Mae West script, followed by a massive publicity campaign for the movie. As long as the box-office receipts were high, Paramount Studios and its New York bankers turned a deaf ear to criticism of her bawdy image; as soon as the grosses fell, however, they backed away from her. Her predictable formula, which never wavered, continued through the decade; its constant repetition became even more hackneyed as time went on.

West's next movie, *Belle of the Nineties* (originally titled *It Ain't No Sin*), reflected West's status as a growing star; the production cost $800,000 and took nearly three months to make. She wrote

the story and screenplay and Leo McCarey directed it. West
wanted Duke Ellington and his band to be in the picture, but
first she had to overcome Paramount's objections to the cost of
that idea. She persisted and prevailed. The film grossed $2 mil-
lion and became one of the five top money makers of 1934. The
Chicago *Tribune* featured five color photos from the movie in its
July 8, 1934, entertainment section and declared that West's
Belle was responsible for the Code. West pooh-poohed that idea
and insisted, as she had done in the old vaudeville days in New
Haven, that it's not what you say but how you say it that counts.

The movie was set in the 1890s, West's favorite period, in New
Orleans. She played Ruby Carter, the "most talked-about
woman in America," as the marquee outside the theater declared in the opening scene. As usual, there were adoring men
surrounding her, witty one-liners, and the triumph of vice over
virtue. The boxer Tiger Kid, Ruby's lover, was advised by his
manager not to see so much of her, as she distracted him from
the ring. Ruby assured the manager that loving and her "art,"
her singing, were her main interests, which she would always
pursue. West sang "St. Louis Woman," "Memphis Blues,"
"My Old Flame," and "Troubled Waters" in the film. She reminded everyone: "One bad habit is as good as another" and
"the man who hesitates lasts." Additional witticisms included:
"It's better to be looked over than overlooked" and "a man in
the house is worth two in the street." Ruby noted that there were
two kinds of men that she liked: foreign and domestic. She leveled the villain with this jibe: "His mother should have thrown
him away and kept the stork." Andre Sennwald, the *New York
Times* critic, thought there were gags for every taste: "Her ser-
pentine gowns, hayloft coiffure and hour-glass figure insure her
against neglect." The *Variety* critic considered the movie a
second-act vaudeville routine, "a comedienne with a straight."

The censor cut a number of the most explicit scenes between
Ruby and the Tiger Kid, including a bedroom scene. Further, a
wedding ceremony was added to sanction their behavior. Although West believed that the woman should always get the guy

of her choice at the end of the movie without any strings at-
tached, the Hays Office insisted upon tying the couple with
marital strings. Her demeanor throughout the movie, however,
assured her viewers that her taste in men was insatiable and not
to be contained by marriage.

By the end of 1934, West had made four films, with the three
in which she starred becoming box-office successes. Her desires,
ambitions, and potential for superstardom, she assumed, were
limitless. In 1933, a year in which, because of the depression, a
fourth of the work force was unemployed, Mae West reported
earnings of $229,840; the following year she earned $344,160,
and in 1935 she earned $480,833. The federal government bene-
fited from her high earnings: she paid the Internal Revenue
Service $234,000 in 1935 (the high tax resulted from her self-
employed status), and the state of California $50,050. Mae net-
ted a mere $155,050, but even that was twice the salary of the
president of the United States. Publisher William Randolph
Hearst, who had instructed all of his newspaper editors to say
little about Mae West and to be sure that whatever was reported
was negative, bristled at the financial comparison some assidu-
ous reporters made: West was the highest-paid woman in 1935,
and Hearst was the highest-paid man. When asked what he
thought of that, Hearst refused to comment. Though Hearst's
private life was not beyond reproach, his public stance was as an
upholder of community values; values scoffed at, he thought by
Mae West.

Public opinion, good and bad, remained focused upon Mae
West, and she loved it. A natural publicity seeker, she knew in-
stinctively that public notice is essential for success in a media-
dominated society, which America was becoming. Even then,
people remembered the brand names they had seen advertised
incessantly, and they went to the movies featuring the star they
had read about regularly in the newspapers and magazines.
Mae West's critics as well as other fans contributed to her popularity. Every time Will Hays or Joseph Breen spoke against her
films, they promoted them; thus she received an astounding

quantity of unpaid publicity. West never endorsed any product and sued anyone who used her name without permission; she guarded her celebrity. Whenever she appeared or promoted herself, that was proper representation; however, if anyone else tried to use her image, that was exploitation.

In the 1930s, amidst lots of publicity, West continued to pursue her interest in boxing and wrestling matches—and the men who participated in them. Her escorts to these events included Gorilla Jones, a black boxer who won the middleweight title during this period, Vincent Lopez, a heavyweight wrestling champion, and Chalky Wright, a featherweight champion whom she managed. West liked muscular men, ostensibly as athletes and as lovers; heavyweights and featherweights, black and white, all were included in her entourage of companions and admirers. "A man and a woman in love," she later wrote, "commit no sin if their codes are decent and they are honest only to two people: each other." She also wrote: "I kept no records of my emotional life—the score never interested me—only the game."

While leading an active social life, West also continued the hectic pace of movie making. In West's 1935 film, *Going to Town,* she played Cleo Borden, a social climber who wanted to enter high society and to mock it at the same time. Although the movie's opening scenes were in the American West, Cleo traveled to Buenos Aires and then England before the movie ended. Even her admiring critics found this movie wanting. Although it possessed some of the formulaic West ingredients—the songs, the swagger, and the adoring males—its plot was highly improbable and the one-liners too few to sustain the humor. West sang "He's a Bad, Bad Man but He's Good for Me" and "Love is Love in any Woman's Heart." Though the movie was not a blockbuster, it made a modest sum for the studio. It was not clear whether West was losing her touch or whether this one film was a temporary setback.

West's career recovered somewhat in 1936 with *Klondike Annie,* directed by Raoul Walsh early in his distinguished career. The film became another favorite of West's fans. Even today movie historians place *Klondike* high in the canon of West's films. The original story, screenplay, and dialogue were all credited to Mae West, though other writers, including the humorist S. J. Perelman, contributed "story ingredients" and dialogue. West played Rose Carlton, the Frisco Doll. Rose began the movie as the kept woman of Chan Lo, a gangster in San Francisco's Chinatown, from whom she escaped, boarding a boat to Alaska. The publicity read: "She met the Frozen North—Red Hot!" On board ship, Rose met Annie, a missionary who personified purity. "Too many girls follow the line of least resistance," Annie said, and Rose replied: "Yeah, but a good line is hard to resist." Annie died on board ship and Rose assumed her clothing and identity so that she could start a new life in a new environment without any taint of her past to inhibit her future.

In Alaska, Rose generally behaved more like a settlement-house worker than a floozy, but the story line offended the conservatives, who thought West was mocking religious people. The plot frustrated Mae's fans, as it had been so toned down by the censors that her famous bawdiness was severely restrained. Despite the censorship, West was able to issue at least one sharp one-liner: "Between two evils, I always pick the one I have never tried before." She sang "I'm an Occidental woman in an Oriental Mood for Love." Frank Nugent, in the *New York Times,* pronounced *Klondike:* "Neither as healthily rowdy nor as vulgarly suggestive as many of her earlier pictures."

One of the sacred rules of the Production Code was that religion had to be portrayed in a respectable manner and a religious worker could not be seen "as a comic character or as a villain." Further, "no girl or woman portrayed as a religious worker may be characterized in any way which would reflect upon religion." Obviously, Mae West as a former prostitute who assumed the identity of a missionary social worker defied that rule. As one interpreter of the code noted, many people "mistook her [West's] garb to be that of a religious worker, and the songs sung in the Settlement House to be hymns sung by a 'congrega-tion.' It was this impression that created much of the public cen-sure of this picture."

Klondike Annie cost $1 million to produce and, thanks to foreign audiences, made money, though not as much as some of her ear-lier movies. Mae West's conservative critics organized letter writing campaigns to discourage attendance at her movies, film critics wondered how her fans never tired of the predictable plots of every Mae West offering, and vigorous competition from other sex comics and goddesses seemed to cut into her au-dience share. Jean Harlow's films allowed fans to see a beautiful and witty woman exchange lines with romantic heroes while both Marlene Dietrich and Greta Garbo allowed women fans to cry over their romantic losses. Dietrich, also a Paramount star, made *The Devil Is a Woman* in 1935 and heated up the screen with her sexual abandon. Harlow, over at MGM, declared in *China Seas* that she was the "gal that drives men mad!" Being sexually interested, available, and even eager was no longer so shocking to movie audiences. West's distinctiveness, of course, was in her exaggerated, comic style. She parodied sex, male vanity, and virtue. West's bawdiness had a hard time competing with the more subtle eroticism of these sex goddesses.

Romantic movies became fashionable in the mid-1930s and Hollywood studios responded with some of the greatest, most sumptuous films ever made. Garbo as *Camille* (1936) offered movie viewers a gorgeous woman in lovely gowns and settings, with fabulous music and handsome Robert Taylor as the heroic male lead. Mae West's vulgarisms were starting to appear stale to many by this time. *Klondike Annie* was the sixth rendition of the Diamond Lil/Mae West persona; fans, however loyal, may have grown a bit tired of her. The very predictability that had been an asset earlier now became a deficit.

But Mae West refused to accept any advice that she change her image. Ignoring the basic rule in popular culture that change is essential to keep the attention of a fickle audience, Mae West operated on the principal that she, Diamond Lil, the shady lady with the heart of gold, was a classic, a persona that never had to change. Audiences, she believed, would keep coming to see the original Mae West, the unflappable version that endured despite changing fashions. Imitators would fall by the wayside and her fans would remain everlastingly loyal. West could not image successors or clever deviations from the theme she presented. Her focus remained on the mirror, the only view she loved.

At this point in her career, West exhibited a rare lapse of judgment; her normally shrewd instincts failed and she did not appreciate the fact that her box office receipts were not growing. While Hollywood enjoyed record attendance levels, Mae West movies were losing their popularity. West blamed those around her. In 1936, neither she nor Paramount Studios were happy with the way things were going. Ernst Lubitsch had become production chief at the studio and he neither liked nor trusted Mae West. They probably did not understand each other either. When Lubitsch told her: "In every story there must be parts for two players, like Romeo and Juliet," she retorted: "that was Shakespeare's technique, but it ain't mine." Lubitsch had a reputation for making sophisticated, witty comedies about marital misunderstandings, and he viewed West as a caricature of the genre. West, on the other hand, was accustomed to working with admirers and with no other stars in the movie. She did not appreciate assertive directors who gave firm direction and expected the star to be compliant and cooperative. West wanted to cancel her contract; an agreement was reached whereby she left the studio and made films with producer Emanuel Cohen, while Paramount continued to act as distributor. In this way, Paramount had none of the production costs or headaches of making a West film, but continued to market, advertise, and distribute the movies through its many theaters around the country. This agreement seemed to please all parties involved.

West favored directors who followed her lead. Although Raoul Walsh, Leo McCarey, and Henry Hathaway all developed major reputations in Hollywood later on, their work with

Mae West came early in their careers. Eager to please and to succeed in the precarious politics of Hollywood, they were willing to allow West a great deal of latitude. Later generations of directors, as well as established directors of her day, were not so compliant. Lubitsch prided himself on his well-scripted stories and his cosmopolitan treatment of love, romance, and adultery. Mae West's persistent one-liners appeared hackneyed and overdone to his European sensibility. She, however, never chose to work with a bossy director. After all, a movie could only tolerate one boss, and that job was already taken by her.

In November 1936, eight months after *Klondike Annie, Go West, Young Man* was released. This was the first Emanuel Cohen production under the Major Pictures imprint and Paramount distribution system. On the surface, the movie looked like most West vehicles: it featured a large cast and an orchestra, this time Xavier Cugat's. West was credited with writing the screenplay, which was based upon a popular play called *Personal Appearance.* She starred as Mavis Arden, a movie star, and never seemed to stop wiggling her way across the screen. Although the *New York Times* critic liked it, the moralists did not. The film had been subjected to heavy editing by the Hays Office, but after its release, many still found it objectionable. The California Congress of Parents and Teachers said: "It is destructive of ethical standards, somewhat demoralizing, and totally lacking in charm." The Southern California Council of Federated Church Women said: "A burlesque on Mae West by Mae West herself." And the General Federation of Women's Clubs echoed the sentiment: "It is replete with sly innuendoes and daring vulgarities, cheaply entertaining."

The one-liners were few. "A thrill a day keeps the chill away" was the best Westism in the movie. The critics seemed to consider her either crude or a self-parody by this time. Similarly, moviegoers seemed to be divided into two camps: uncritical fans who enjoyed her predictable characterization, or detractors who no longer attended her movies but felt free to criticize them. Mae West's enormous ego convinced her that her portrayal was funny, entertaining, and worthy of a large following, but she blamed poor script opportunities in Hollywood. Although she prided herself on reworking every script she accepted, she claimed that there were fewer vehicles to consider. She had been interested in bringing the historical Queen Catherine the Great of Russia to the screen, but the studio considered it too expensive a project. Also, Paramount had already produced Marlene Dietrich's version of Catherine in *The Scarlet Empress* (1934), and they saw no need for another film on the same topic.

By the end of 1936, Mae West had been working steadily in Hollywood for five years; when she was not filming a movie, she was either working on a script or traveling around the country promoting a new release. In 1937, she found the work schedule slowed because of a lack of good scripts and a shaky financial basis for her ambitious plans. Independent producer Emanuel Cohen did not have the resources of Paramount Studios, and although he was generally supportive of West and her projects, he urged caution. The atmosphere in movieland was growing chilly for Mae West, and although she was to continue in the movie business for a few more years, her film ideas no longer received instant approval by the power brokers. The smiling and agreeable executives that had greeted her after the enormous success of *She Done Him Wrong* were no longer in view.

Yet the sky had not fallen. In 1937 The Benevolent Order of Santa Clauses announced Mae West and Shirley Temple had tied for first place as their favorite movie stars. West still sparked in fan heaven. She worked on another movie, and in October 1937 began production on *Every Day's a Holiday,* in which she played two parts, Peaches O'Day and Mademoiselle Fifi. Louis Armstrong and his band also appeared in the film.

Before the scheduled release of the movie in January 1938, Paramount's publicity people thought that, in addition to West's personal tour, she should go on a radio show to promote the movie. Mae West had never been on the radio before, and her critics feared that she would corrupt the airwaves, just as she had the silver screen. In early 1934, there had been rumors that West was to appear on a radio show. According to one account, she had asked for $7,500 per broadcast; the station had countered with an offer of $5,000. Allegedly, they settled for $6,600 a show. But something happened and the deal fell apart. "It is rumored that her prospective sponsors got chills and fever trying to think up ways of getting her rough-and-ready chatter from offending the nation's blue-noses," reported Margaret Dale in *Radio Stars* (March 1934). Her December 1937 appearance on the very popular Chase and Sanborn Hour, starring Edgar Bergen and his puppet, Charlie McCarthy, confirmed the censors' fears. It caused such a sensation that she was not to appear on the radio for twelve years.

West later claimed that she had not even looked at the script before air time; Don Ameche, the show's announcer, who appeared in the skit with her, recalled that she had been cooperative and pleasant to work with. In any case, the skit, a comic rendition of the Adam and Eve story, sounds mildly amusing today, and from the reaction of the small studio audience (as heard on record), the laughter came at the right times. But the public reaction was overwhelmingly negative. Congressmen threatened to revoke the license of KFI, the NBC station that broadcast the show, and other legislators said that they would break up RCA's monopoly of radio stations. J. Walter Thompson, the advertising agency for Chase and Sanborn, publicly apologized and assured audiences that they would monitor all future material carefully to ensure its propriety.

What was the fuss all about? The skit opened with Adam and Eve playing cards with a deck of fig leafs. Eve was bored, while Adam was happy to hang out in Eden indefinitely. She kept insisting that "a girl has to have a little fun some time" and that "there is no future under a fig tree." Eve also insisted that she was a "lady with big ideas" and that she needed a "chance to expand [her] personality." Adam reminded her that they had a lease and that it could not be broken. She instructed him to break the lease because "it's too safe, it's disgusting." When he reminded her that she came from his rib and should therefore be obedient, she replied: "A rib once and now I'm beefing." As the conversation continued, Eve discovered that there was one way that they could get out of the lease, but Adam refused to tell what it was. She tricked him and discovered that they were prohibited from eating apples from the tree protected by a fence.

Adam went off fishing and Eve planned her escape strategy. She climbed over the fence, gathered some apples and made applesauce. Upon Adam's return, she presented him with the new food and assured him that he would like it. Adam ate the applesauce and she remarked: "I am the first woman to have her own way and the snake will take the rap for it." After eating, Adam looked at Eve in a new way; they kiss. The innocent Adam asked what that was and she replied: "The original kiss." End of skit. Laughter and applause came from the audience.

Mae West was puzzled by the intense antagonism the skit engendered. To 1990s listeners, the skit appears to be mildly amusing and clever. Mae West's Eve was in character both with her public persona of a take-charge 1930s woman and contemporary standards of an independent woman. Adam was characterized as "long, lazy, and lukewarm," whereas Eve was petite, active, and passionate. Eve was imaginative and daring while Adam was complacent and unadventurous. The sex-role reversal was humorous and in keeping with West's image. There were no double entendres, no obvious vulgarisms. Because Mae West could be heard and not seen, most of the crude sexual gimmickry that she was known for was missing. Her real power could not be captured on the radio, and yet the censors both feared and deplored her.

Surely it was the irreverent treatment of the Bible, the Genesis story of Adam and Eve, that infuriated the traditionalists. Although West did not take the Lord's name in vain, she took His version of the conditions under which the first man and woman left the Garden of Eden lightly. West's well-known reputation for joking about sex, combined with her willingness to spoof a sacred subject, were clearly too much for those who considered their role to be guardians of public morality. The Catholic

Church as well as various evangelical Protestant churches considered Mae West a dangerous and obnoxious example of America's decline in morality.

Conventional wisdom affirms that all publicity, good, bad, or indifferent, helps the cause, the product, or the personality, or so it had always seemed in the case of Mae West. But for the first time that philosophy backfired; _Every Day's A Holiday_ suffered from the adverse publicity engendered by West's appearance on the Chase and Sanborn Hour. West, undeterred, planned her personal appearance tour for the movie as if nothing had happened. Her appearance, which preceded the movie's showing, consisted of a twenty-minute routine in which she sang some songs surrounded by six men, all over six feet tall, wearing top hats and tail coats. Eight shows a day were planned, an ambitious and arduous undertaking, but consistent with West's love of a live audience and belief in giving her fans their money's worth.

Lionel Newman, the musical conductor, accompanied West and her entourage on the winter 1938 tour. He remembered the experience with a certain amount of awe. Mae West, he recounted, was totally self-absorbed, always acting and never letting down her guard. She received many letters from fans, including some lewd ones. Newman said: "She talked turkey, and she adored getting letters, the dirtier the better."

The tour was a failure. _Every Day's a Holiday_ was the first Mae West film to lose money. The movie, like its predecessors, suffered at the hands of the censor. And this time the damage from the adverse publicity, the moralists, the censors, and the inherent weakness of the material made for a dismal showing.

Mae West continued to behave as if she did not know what all the fuss was about. She always maintained that she controlled the censors, not the other way around. Some of the lines cut from _Every Day's a Holiday_ included: "I wouldn't even lift my veil for that guy," and "I wouldn't let him touch me with a ten-foot pole." However, the censors ignored Peaches O'Day's response to the question of whether she kept a diary: "I always say, keep a diary and some day it'll keep you." Her quipping ability was also evident when it was mentioned that Peaches had been arrested twenty-five times in the past six months. Peaches' reply: "Well, no woman's perfect."

Every Day's a Holiday was the last film West made with Emanuel Cohen and her last film for Paramount. By 1938, West's drawing power, an unusual combination of predictability and fresh twists, seemed to fail her. Her 1930s films had provided needed fantasy, escape, and comic relief for a tired and often desperate population. Laughter was good, especially if you were unemployed. When people felt restricted and trapped by circumstances beyond their control, Mae West was footloose and fancy free. She was a woman alone, making it on her own. There were other movie stars of the period who conveyed much the same impression: surely Katharine Hepburn, Barbara Stanwyck, and Bette Davis fit into the same category, but none did it with the obvious good humor in every one of their movies. Both Hepburn and Stanwyck made some stylish comedies in the 1930s, but they did not play a sex goddess who spoofed sex. They were independent women who also were sexually attractive, but they never joked about that quality the way Mae West did.

For the first time since she arrived in Hollywood seven years earlier, Mae West had no contract or commitment to a studio. Her suggestions for film ideas found no interested takers. Thus, in 1939, when Universal Studios approached her to appear in a movie with the comic W. C. Fields costarring, West was ready to agree. This action was unusual for her in that she had never before allowed another star to receive equal billing. But the studio allowed each star to write her or his own part. The result was *My Little Chickadee,* a rather jumbled story that looked more like a series of skits than a coherent narrative.

West played Flower Belle Lee and Fields was Cuthbert J. Twillie; the film had a Western setting but was filmed in the studio and not on location. Each star wrote good lines for herself or himself, but made little effort to interact. West's one-liners were still in evidence. When asked what kind of woman she was, she replied: "Too bad I can't give out samples." When someone remarked that spring was the time for love, she quipped: "What's wrong with the rest of the year?"

West did not enjoy the making of *My Little Chickadee.* Fields had a well-deserved reputation as a heavy drinker and Mae West could not abide alcohol; she had written into the contract the provision that if she smelled liquor on his breath, he would have to leave the set. Fields behaved himself and only had to be excused from one day of filming. Mae West was not used to sharing the spotlight with another star. Except for young Cary Grant, in the days before he became a star, she had never had a leading man who competed with her for center stage. W. C. Fields was her first, and last, serious contender for the star position. West once said that she needed three men in a movie with her: one for comedy, one for drama, and one for romance. Fields may have qualified on the first count, but there were no other men in the movie to fill the other positions. The critics agreed with Mae West's negative appraisal. Frank Nugent of the *New York Times* said: "Miss West's humor, like Miss West herself, appears to be growing broader with the years and begins to turn upon the lady; it's one thing to burlesque sex and quite another to be burlesqued by it." Because of the combined presence of West and Fields in the movie, however, the box office response was good.

Ironically, later generations would point to *My Little Chickadee* as a favorite example of 1930s comedies. However, that evaluation may be based as much on Fields' presence in the movie as Mae West's. Classic or essential Mae West can better be observed in *She Done Him Wrong, I'm No Angel,* or *Klondike Annie.* To later viewers, having two icons of Hollywood appear in the same movie, each throwing off the quips that had established their earlier reputations, made the movie worthwhile. To contemporary followers of all West's movies, this 1940 entry was lackluster.

By her own account, West's spiritual searching for fulfillment increased in 1940 and 1941, precisely when her movie career seemed headed downward. This seemingly self-confident woman sought guidance from mystical and parapsychology practitioners in Los Angeles, a haven for new and experimental philosophies and therapies. Although claiming to be a rationalist and a skeptic, she opened herself to alternative ways of understanding reality. Among the unorthodox thinkers she became acquainted with were Sri Deva Ram Sukul, whom she had first met in 1928, Dr. Frank Buchman, a self-styled religious leader who headed the Moral Rearmament movement on the West Coast, and the Reverend Thomas Jack Kelly of the Spiritualist Church of Life in Buffalo, New York.

Mae West was interested in seances and Kelly's ability to practice extra-sensory perception (ESP). Sri Deva Ram Sukul also held seances. West was unwilling to deny their potential for success. She claimed that these men helped her to develop her spiritual side, for which she was grateful. Of course she was not alone in California or the nation. The need for answers to the mystery of life and to the practical problems Americans faced seemed pressing indeed. The depression had not ended for many by 1940, and war clouds in Europe suggested new catastrophes to come. Although West showed little interest in world affairs or economics, she was concerned about her immediate future. As her movie career was clearly in decline, the possibilities for the future seemed cloudy.

Mae West became a follower of the Reverend Kelly's philosophy. She decided to devote six months to her spiritual life and to discover whether there was a hereafter. Though she never reached a firm conclusion, Kelly became a friend to whom she turned at various times in the future. West's public image as a wisecracking lover of life never changed, but she clearly explored a more serious side of her personality in private. In her 1959 autobiography, she described these experiences in a matter-of-fact manner and categorized them as consistent with her continual interest in self-discovery. Because she devoted so much time to herself, it was in character to devote herself to learning whether the inimitable Mae West would exist in the same form in future lives. She was definitely not interested in being reincarnated as another person.

Mae West received more dubious publicity in 1941 and 1942. Her long-lost husband, vaudevillian Frank Wallace, whom she had married in 1911 and left after four months when their careers took them in different directions, reappeared in 1941 and sued her for $1,000 a month in separation maintenance. The newspapers had a field day. In 1937 Wallace had gotten a judge to recognize him as West's legal husband, a fact that Mae had vociferously denied for years. When Wallace returned to court in 1941 seeking financial support, she took action and countersued him for divorce. That lawsuit came before the court in July 1942. Wallace retaliated by naming six men, including her longtime business manager, Jim Timony, as correspondents in his divorce suit. In addition to the inherent sensationalism of the material, the reporters discovered additional dirt when it was revealed that two of the correspondents, Kid Twist Reles and Bugsy Siegel, were alleged gangsters associated with Murder, Inc.

West, in typical fashion, turned the media event into an opportunity for her to remind the public of her unique personality. She smiled demurely for the cameras, reveled in the numerous interviews, and told Robert Rhodes in the *American Weekly* that "maybe we owe 'em a lovin' but not a livin.' " West used the episode to lecture on man-woman relationships, her favorite subject, and asserted that too many men tried to live off wealthy women. "We've tried a new deal in everything else. Let's have a new deal between men and women, husbands and wives," she declared, "I don't hold a grudge against Frankie—but I would just as leave he didn't come up to see me some time. In fact, I do not want to see him any time."

The Heat's On (1943), West's last picture of the period, was an unpleasant experience. "I'll never make a picture again just for the sake of making a picture," she later declared. In this movie, she played Fay Lawrence, yet another version of Diamond Lil. As West put it: "I gave the role every different shading and meaning I could. I honestly think I have exhausted all its possibilities." This was Mae West's eighth film version of the good-hearted gal from the Gay Nineties, and though she was to continue portraying Lil on the stage, in night clubs, and in rare radio and television appearances, it was the final time she played Lil on film. *The Heat's On* was a two-hour movie with West on screen for only twenty-four minutes. The lines were flat and it seemed evident to most viewers that West did not have her heart in the enterprise.

It was during the 1930s that the British navy named their inflatable life jackets Mae Wests, because of their resemblance to West's outstanding physical features, and her name and persona seemed permanently emblazoned upon the imaginations of the America of that decade. Despite her faded film career, Mae West was not ready to rest on her laurels in 1943; she was still energetic, and ambitious, and eager to continue performing. Now fifty years old and quite wealthy from her real estate investments and earnings, she was living in a sumptuously decorated apartment in Hollywood and a luxurious house in Santa Monica. However, retirement did not even enter her mind. She looked for new vistas to conquer or, in the case of Catherine the Great, an old project to rekindle.

CHAPTER FOUR

I Like Two Kinds of Men: Foreign and Domestic

1944–1964

The Empress of Sex was determined to become the Empress of All the Russias. Movie making became a memory as Mae West turned her Catherine the Great idea into a theatrical play. Catherine, according to West, was her kind of woman. Allegedly, she had had three hundred lovers while she ruled her eighteenth-century empire; but, as West told her audience after completing a performance of her dramatization, which she called *Catherine Was Great,* "I did the best I could in a couple of hours." There were only fourteen lovers in West's three-act play. Catherine, she said, was "a Slavic-Germanic Diamond Lil, just as low in vivid sexuality but on a higher plane of authority." True to form, her audiences enjoyed her spoof of the historical queen, but the critics hated it. *Variety* summed it up: "Critics cold but b.o. [box office] hot."

Catherine Was Great was produced by Michael Todd, who was known for spending large amounts of money on his productions. He spared no expense for this nonmusical play; published accounts reported a record expenditure for 1944—$100,000. Everyone noticed the lavish costumes and the elaborate sets when the play opened on Broadway at the Shubert Theater on

August 2, 1944. West played it straight for the first two performances and received a tepid response from the audience; reports
claimed that Todd then instructed her to play her role comically
and not do a poor imitation of dramatic actress Helen Hayes.
West obliged, camped up her performance, and ensured her
success. She stayed on Broadway for seven months before taking
the show on the road. Despite the popular response, the production never returned Todd's large investment. West, however,
prospered: she received a generous salary and enjoyed perpetu-
ating her image of the sexually insatiable woman—on and off
the stage. She told one interviewer: "Sometimes it seems to me
I've known so many men that the FBI ought to come to me first
to compare fingerprints."

By all accounts, World War II had no impact on the personality and actions of Mae West. She blithely continued to do what
she did best. While many male stars went to war and Hollywood
made patriotic movies, West left movieland with no regrets and
returned to the live stage where she had always been well treated
and where she could hear the direct responses of her fans. Patrons had more money to spend; unemployment disappeared as
the country prepared for and entered the war, and many people
began to accumulate wartime savings. Producer Todd could
raise large sums of money to mount lavish productions such as
Catherine Was Great because producers had surplus cash and audiences eagerly sought diverting experiences during the stressful
days of the war and the immediate postwar period.

Mae West, oblivious to the critics' negative response to
Catherine Was Great, did what she loved best—she toured with the
play, enjoying such big cities as Chicago for four-week engagements. Her personal appearances brought out her old fans and
allowed members of the younger generation to make her ac-
quaintance for the first time (she had not been seen in a play
since 1931). Some of the critics who reviewed her play, in fact,
commented that they had not been born when West began her
show business career. Each critic preceded his or her review of
the play with a summary of West's career, thereby reminding

readers of her legendary status in show business and her amazing endurance. They contributed to the image of her as the sex
symbol of multiple generations. During the mid-1940s, West expanded her fan base to include a third generation.

At this stage in her career, Mae West achieved cult status to
her perennial fans, became a star to the new generation that met
her for the first time in the theater and later the night club, and
was a celebrity to all who followed the mass media. Each of these
roles featured different aspects of West's personality: the cult
fans craved the predictable smirk and the great one-liners; the
newly initiated admired the novelty of an aging sex goddess who
could still swagger across the stage; the reader of popular culture magazines or newspaper articles was amused by her avid
publicity seeking. Her longevity, combined with her supreme
self-confidence, made her audacious remarks from the 1920s
seem funny and incongruous in the 1950s; the humor, rather
than the bawdiness, moved to the forefront. She had no equal as
a cult star, a star, and a celebrity all in one, still working the
crowds, still granting interviews, and still doing live theater.

Her frequent interviews contributed to her celebrity status.
She described how she had always been in show business, had
always had a healthy interest in sex, and had always had complete confidence in her ability to succeed. Although in the 1940s
she was in her fifties, West's appearance had not changed appre-
ciably since the 1920s, though a tight corset was needed to preserve the image. She did have to watch her weight, she admitted,
but insisted that she still weighed 120 pounds. She still wore high
heels to raise her 5′ to a more commanding height. Her skin remained smooth, and she continued to wear false eyelashes and
heavy makeup. Many interviewers swore that they could not de-
tect any face-lifting scars on her neck or around her ears, though
they looked for them.

Although most theater critics, even the most charitable ones,
did not have any kind words to say about *Catherine Was Great,* a
few intellectuals, most notably Stark Young in *The New Republic*

and Kappo Phelan in *Commonweal,* found some redeeming features in West's portrayal. "What is perhaps less obvious," Phelan noted, "is that she is, as well as an American structure, an
actress of uncommon skill, capable of the most subtle timing,
the projection of the slightest nuance." Young reminded his
readers that "Miss West's acting is strictly presentational.
Which means that she frankly presents herself and the dramatic
moment as herself, as theater, as a show." He found her persona
"abstract" and her humor "healthy and masculine, more bar-
room than glandular." Finally, Young defined her appeal as her
ability to create "a howling, diverting mythology of glamour;
you watch her as you watch an animal in a cage, tigress or cinna-
mon bear."

Stark Young was not the first critic, nor would he be the last,
to try to explain the basis of Mae West's power and lasting appeal. Whether many of her fans could articulate the reasons for
their willingness to attend a fifty-one-year-old's portrayal of a
Russian queen is not clear. One fan's explanation appeared in
the *Brooklyn Eagle.* After the theater critic Arthur Pollock had
bashed the play, Liboria Romano, who had been at the 1944
opening night in New York, wrote an indignant letter to him,
which he graciously reprinted in his column:

> First of all, because it is a feast of opulence and beauty for eyes
> weary with this worn-out war-torn world. The settings are 'out of
> this world' and worth paying a few dollars to see.... What I like
> about this play is exactly that there isn't any dirt in it.... Mae
> West's talent makes of the audience not merely spectators—they
> participate. Her sensuous way of caressing each word, no matter
> how banal, makes the audience see so much filth in their minds they
> don't have to have it handed to them by Mae. Yes sir, the big girl is
> Wonderful, and from now on she has an enthusiastic follower and
> fan in yours truly.

Mae West's Brooklyn fan captured an important West quality
that has been referred to in every generation: bawdy singers in

vaudeville and burlesque were very explicit in their sexual references; in a later generation, rock singers leave little to the imagination; but Mae West teased sexual themes and conveyed her
meaning through a gesture, a leer, or a swagger of the hips. As
she reminded her audiences regularly, it was the way she said
something more than what she said that evoked the desired response. Further, audiences were never quite sure whether West
was kidding about her overwhelming sexual appeal, whether she
knew her exaggerated claims and gestures were silly, or whether
she was sincere. The preservation of this mystery persisted for
over fifty years. She never let on to interviewers or audiences
what her real feelings were.

As evidence of how seriously she took her portrayal of
Catherine, she told all interested parties that she had had Russian books translated into English so that she could learn all
there was to know about her subject. When told by one reporter
that historians did not agree with her interpretation of one Pu-
gachev, she blithely disagreed and moved on to other matters.
She claimed that her rendering of the material "will show how
she [Catherine] ruled the country with one hand, and men with
the other." In one of the humorous interchanges in the play,
Catherine tells Prince Potemkin, with whom she was discussing
the Turkish situation: "The Turkish situation interests me
greatly, Prince Potemkin. Come around, and we'll talk Turkey."

West's obvious spoofing of the subject, her clear interest in
shaping all material to her central theme, seemed to elude the
critics. They kept asking serious questions while she wise-
cracked. "Russia needs her men," she concluded one interview,
"I need them, I cannot spare a single one more than is necessary." Truth and fancy always mingled easily in West's mind.
Any gullible reporter who believed that she had read endless historical works to check on the accuracy of her rendition should
have returned to journalism school.

Even when the critics hated her work, they could not stop
writing about her. John Chapman of the New York *Daily News*

found *Catherine Was Great* dreadful, and he wondered in print why it continued to attract an audience. Jim Timony, still West's manager, was quoted as saying that 85 percent of the audience consisted of women; this gave Chapman what he thought was the clue to the play's success: "... women like dirt more than men do.... There is a great deal of bedroom talk and Miss West is smirking most of the time. It isn't very clever dirt and it really isn't at all shocking—but it's the kind women want, apparently. They seem to be simple souls." How readers reacted to this dubious conclusion is not known.

After the Broadway close of the play, West took it on tour for most of 1945. At the same time, she was planning the revival of the original 1928 version of her greatest play, *Diamond Lil.* She also wrote another play, *Come On Up...Ring Twice,* which she performed in summer-stock playhouses in Montclair, New Jersey, Long Island, Long Beach, California, and Chicago. Always mindful of press and audience reaction, West kept a scrapbook of newspaper clippings, particularly the favorable ones. In her 1959 autobiography, *Goodness Had Nothing to Do with It,* she quoted the Chicago *Herald-American's* review of *Come On Up:* "Miss West is an American institution. She is like Chicago—brazen, colorful, alive and vulgar, if you wish."

West's constant activity, her willingness, even her eagerness, to remain in the public eye, were nothing less than remarkable, a fact commented upon by all observers. After all, she was getting older. When she went to London with the revival of *Diamond Lil* in September 1947, she was fifty-four years old, not an old woman by 1990s standards, but surely an older woman by 1947 criteria. Interviewers always asked her what she thought of the latest glamour girls in Hollywood. She pretended not to know who Betty Grable, Rita Hayworth, and Lana Turner were. No younger competition existed in her mind, just as she had never recognized any competition from peers. West continued to believe that her loyal, and growing, audience gladly welcomed her every appearance. She could not disappoint them.

They wanted to see the inimitable Mae West in her most enduring play, as well as in any new offering she deemed worthy of
their attention.

Mae West loved England and the English returned the affec-
tion. She took *Diamond Lil* to Birmingham and Blackpool before
opening in London at the Prince of Wales Theatre on January
25, 1948. The demand for tickets was so great that she did two
shows a night (Mae West never did matinees). In contrast to the
cool reception of *Catherine Was Great* by the New York critics, that
of the London writers was warm; they loved it and Mae West.
Leonard Moseley of *The Daily Express* said: "Her fellow actors
hardly matter. But she, herself, is a Restoration comedy rolled
into one body—earthy, happy and outspoken. Shocked, me?
No, I just like her." The *Times* of London critic wrote: "She puts
across her own kind of audacity with good timing and a shrewd
sense of its essential absurdity."

After eight months in England, West returned to the United
States in May 1948. She was on a roll and decided to tour with
Diamond Lil in this country. When she opened in New York in
February 1949, many of the critics looked up their newspaper's
1928 review to compare the original reaction to the play with
their opinion twenty-one years later. Generally, they were
amazed at how resilient both Mae West and Diamond Lil were
and how they shared the original enthusiasm, both for the play
and Mae West. Their surprised, almost awed response assured
another successful run, although even their displeasure probably would not have deterred fans.

Brooks Atkinson, the venerable *New York Times* drama critic,
went to see *Diamond Lil* on November 30, 1948, at the Montclair
Theater in New Jersey before its New York run and then again
when it opened in early February at the Coronet Theater. He
advised his readers that "...Mae is holding out all right, and
is, in fact, become a part of American folklore, like the minstrel
show and burlesque," words that contributed to her growing
legend as an American institution. He continued: "She dresses
exclusively in the gigantic flowing hats and the flouncing trains

of fleshpots iniquity and packs quite a lot of billowing flesh inside them. She is always in motion like the serpent in the
garden—wriggling, waving, swaying." Atkinson assured his
readers that "although her subject is sex, she manages to keep
the sexiness out of it by burlesquing it outrageously." He concluded that "Mae is an original, unclassified phenomenon." Although defining her as unclassified, he wrote many words to try
to define her, as did many of his contemporaries as well as writers of subsequent generations.

Harold Clurman, an experienced theatrical director, also
marveled at Mae West's amazing talent. In an article in *The
New Yorker,* he labeled her a "consummate technician...with...
a remarkable mimic sense and great guile in self-display." After
spending a good deal of space to explain the inexplicable, he
ended: "She gives the public what it wants: a glittering facsimile
of what it craves and, through laughter, a means of keeping itself
free of what it fears. She horses around with sex so that we can
have our cake and not eat it." In an age when sexual discussion
and display were becoming more public, Clurman's and Atkinson's attempts to understand West's popularity demonstrated
the problematic nature of her appeal. In earlier periods, when
Victorian morality still held sway, West's brand of suggestive
sexuality was outrageous and offensive enough to land her in jail
in 1928; but by 1949, the shackles of censorship were loosening,
or so thought the critics. How could Mae West's version of sexual relations, dressed in 1890s costumes, still find an audience?
Perhaps, as Clurman suggested, it was the very fact that West
made fun of a subject that was still fraught with forbidden elements that ensured her continued success. Apparently, censorship still lived.

Besides the critics who found a brilliant exposé of sexual mo-
res in Mae West's performances, there were critics who had
never seen her before and attended a performance of *Diamond
Lil* just to understand what all the fuss was about. One writer
who saw her for the first time in 1951 noted that the play was "a
creaky melodrama full of hokum which, without Miss West, no

intelligent person could, for one moment, take seriously." But, he concluded, "like Chinatown and Grant's Tomb, Miss West is something to see, once anyway." Unconsciously perhaps, this critic went to the theater expecting to see a fresh theatrical talent, a star. His disappointment is understandable because he judged her by the wrong standards. Age seemed to determine the critics' views; younger writers tended to wonder what all the fuss was about while older commentators, such as Harold Clurman, tended to admire the durability of Mae West. The *Commonweal* critic admitted in 1951 to a broken heart:

> Until now the mere mention of Miss West has been enough to fill me with an immense good humor; on seeing her in the at present too ample flesh, I am left with the impression that once upon a time a very limited talent stumbled, perhaps by accident, into some remarkably funny effects which have since been parlayed into something far beyond their intrinsic comic value. All right, I'm a cad. But a dream has been shattered, and I'm bitter.

Many long-time admirers and enthusiastic new fans, however, continued to fill the seats for *Diamond Lil* and leave the theater happy, having seen the legend in person. From 1948 through 1951, West toured with the play, including four separate appearances in New York. Always an astute businesswoman, she negotiated a very favorable contract for herself: she earned $1,500 a week and 10 percent of the gross over $20,000. As West told interviewers, she believed in being paid for her efforts. No one, she advised them, should fritter away his or her gifts; they are precious and must be carefully nurtured. West, of course, took her own advice, not only in financial matters but in health concerns as well. She walked regularly, ate moderately (rarely eating meat), and never drank or smoked. Her strict daily regimen reflected her self-involvement; her physical and mental health were her first and last interest. She freely shared her views with reporters and columnists, attributing her ability to perform so effectively in her late fifties to her health habits. By this point in her career, West acknowledged her age, but dismissed it as unimportant. How you feel is what counts, she told everyone, not your chronological age.

Although West always spoke of herself as extremely healthy, she had abdominal problems that required hospitalization in the late 1940s. She later broke her ankle in New York while performing in *Diamond Lil* in 1951; it took many months to heal. Her eyesight was poor, but she was too vain to wear glasses; as a result, she always walked holding her current beau's arm. Throughout the 1950s, whenever she granted an interview in her Ravenswood apartment (the same place she had first rented in 1932), she always sat in a chair with a table next to it on which all of the articles she would need were strategically placed.

Mae West's ego and self-esteem were so high as to seem boundless. Encouraged by interviewers to compare herself to all previous greats, she took the bait and told Lucius Beebe of the New York *Herald Tribune* that she was as longlasting as the great Sarah Bernhardt, who played to the end of her life although she had only one leg. "I'm one up on her right there," West declared, referring to her own two legs. Warming to the subject, she continued: "Diamond Lil is all mine. I'm she. She's I, and in my modest way I consider her a classic. Like Hamlet, sort of, but funnier. I'm permanently typecast and I love every moment of it." Newspaper writers, be they columnists, gossip writers, or show business reporters, begged for opportunities to interview the queen of the one-liner and the greatest self-promoter since P. T. Barnum. Although West had her share of bad publicity, she found more admirers than critics in the press corps.

In her quest for regular media exposure, West returned to radio in 1949. She went on the Chesterfield Supper Club Show, which starred the popular singer Perry Como, in January 1949, her first radio show in twelve years. NBC, which had suffered much criticism for her Eve portrayal on the Chase and Sanborn Hour in 1937, hoped that the censors were napping or that public tastes had become more tolerant. The show was vintage West, with Como fawning all over "Miss West" as she described her perfume, "Panther Passion," as "one whiff and you leap."

When Como declared himself to be a perfect gentleman, West asked: "Which are you? Perfect or a gentleman?"

In February, 1950, she went on his show again, doing a Little Red Riding Hood skit with him. While Como sang: "I'm in the Mood for Love," West replied: "Who isn't?" The theme continued, to everyone's delight. West publicized the tour she was doing of *Diamond Lil,* reminding listeners in Rochester and Toronto to come to see her. She told Perry Como that her fans would be interested in knowing that she was wearing a 30-carat diamond necklace and a 25-carat bracelet. Audience ratings were high, and the censor found nothing objectionable in Mae West's performance.

In the mid-1950s, West continued to believe that her audiences needed constant, or at least regular, exposure to her. Film was no longer a viable medium for her, and though she claimed that she could do revivals of Diamond Lil indefinitely, in 1954 she chose to return to night clubs, where she had not performed since the early 1920s. In the recent past, she had dismissed night clubs because of the eating, drinking, smoking, and talking. But the introduction of an overhead microphone system and the assurance that no food or drink would be served during her performance convinced West that she should return to this venue.

She decided to create a show that appealed to women, rather than to her normal constituency, men. Although she claimed that she had always been sensitive to women's feelings, the new act, first performed in July 1954 at the Sahara Hotel in Las Vegas, was clearly aimed at women; it featured fifteen men, including eight musclemen. Mr. Universe, Mr. America, and other well-built men paraded around the stage showing off their impressive physiques. In the thirty-nine-minute show, the men's parade was followed by West singing as seven men danced around her. The show became an effective spoof of the "girlie" shows that played regularly in Las Vegas and in burlesque houses. Mae West remained the center of male attention, of course, while women members of the audience feasted their eyes on the men. The *Variety* reviewer noted the female ringsiders' "blushing gasps of admiration to the musclemen, while their paunchy and/or anemic escorts cringe before the display of physical excellence."

Mae West's night club act broke new ground in that it gave women an opportunity to view men as sex objects, an unprecedented action. Although West would later take credit for anticipating the feminist movement of the 1960s and 1970s, it is more likely that her innovative act was motivated by novelty and her personal preference. She, after all, liked to look at musclemen and to be surrounded by male admirers. Why not stage a show around this preference? Further, she appreciated the humorous possibilities, bordering on the vulgar, that could be exploited in the night club setting of Las Vegas. Mae West's background in early vaudeville could be recalled; the intimacy of the setting and the high price of the show assured an appreciative and non-censored audience.

Mae West was one month away from her sixty-first birthday when she debuted in *Made in France,* as she called her night club act. From the opening song, "I Like To Do All Day What I Do All Night," until she closed by handing each of the musclemen a key, West leered, sang, and swaggered across the stage. For those old enough to remember, the night club show must have brought back memories of thirty years earlier. The 1954 production, of course, had more elaborate costumes and dancing numbers, but the one-liners and the singularity of the theme were the same as West's vaudeville act in the early 1920s. West sang "Frankie and Johnny" and "Take It Easy, Boys, and Last a Long, Long Time." At one point in the show, the musclemen marched on stage wearing fur capes, turned toward West, and opened their capes; West then made suggestive remarks about their anatomies and the audience roared. In later years, she told reporters that women thanked her for finally giving them a chance to enjoy themselves in a night club.

To the pleasant astonishment of the night club owners and the columnists, the show was an enormous success. Gossip columnist Hedda Hopper, who had many readers, raved about it. "What have the old timers got that the present generation lacks?" she asked, and then answered: "Talent, experience, and know-how. Our girls who think they know how should attend Mae's night school and learn a trick or two." Numerous writers wondered: "How does Mae still do it?" Even West told gossip columnist Earl Wilson that despite all of her past hits, "I never figgered on a success like this."

When West left the Sahara Hotel, she traveled to New York's Latin Quarter, one of the city's finest night spots. The interest was so great that additional shows had to be added and the original four-week commitment was extended to seven weeks. Lou Walters, the club owner, said: "She's done more business than we ever imagined could be done. . . . We'd hold her over for the duration of our seven-year lease if we could." Reporter Gene Knight noted that the line around the Latin Quarter extended out onto the 42nd Street sidewalk and around the corner onto Broadway. "Not all men, either!" He also observed that the applause at the end of her act lasted almost ten minutes. When she reappeared at the Latin Quarter in April 1956, a thousand fans waited to get in opening night. "This gal is show wise," reported Knight, and "if there's any show business trick she doesn't know, it must have been used before she was born. Which was quite a few years ago, honey."

From 1954 to 1959, Mae West appeared in her musclemen show all around the country. She played Copa City in Miami Beach, the Chez Paree in Chicago, the Italian Village in San Francisco, and the Latin Casino in Philadelphia. She interspersed the club engagements with summer-stock performances of her play *Come On Up. . . Ring Twice,* which was also well received. She was indefatigable. "I keep busy," she told Hedda Hopper, "I always have my plays—I'm from legitimate, you know." The audience's applause, the concrete manifestation of her fans' adoration, was tonic to her. She seemed to need the constant reinforcement as much as she needed food.

The act changed during its five-year run; it became racier and raunchier. Columnist Herb Stein said of the show in March 1959: "It's out-and-out raw. . . . Miss West is the mistress of single entendre." Writing in a family newspaper, Stein noted, prevented him from giving his readers details. He told them that although West did not do a striptease, her musclemen, in their loincloths, did, to the oohs and ahs of the women in the audience. He also reported that West did not move around very much, but instead reclined on a chaise lounge. Her dancers and musclemen did all of the work. West's contribution was one-liners: "Rome wasn't built in a daybed," she said; and in an exchange with the men that was supposed to be a TV dream sequence, she is asked: "What is your favorite cigarette?" She replied: "Marijuana." Interviewer: "Do you think all men should smoke marijuana?" Mae: "I say every man should fly for himself." In the show's finale, Stein reported, everyone declared, "Mae West for President," waving placards reading: "West Front Forward," "Best by Test," "No Sin Tax," and "A Man in Every Bed."

Writers clearly loved to describe her shows. Hy Gardner, another New York gossip columnist, wrote: "Miss West, who made sex popular all the way back to when Dr. Kinsey was young enough to sneak into Minsky's to conduct some early research, still sells the old commodity." Reporters searched for new ways to describe the same old act. But often they just resorted to writing the equivalent of a sigh and a shrug, wondering aloud how she did it. No one was quite sure what her appeal was, but everyone saw that she still had it. Louis Sobel claimed: "For at all times there was a feeling that even at her bawdiest, Mae was winking—as if to indicate that actually she is a chaste, sedate spinster woman engaged in her life's work of a tongue-in-cheek satirization of the eternal by-play between the sexes."

In 1954, one newspaper account claimed that Mae West had the largest fan club of any star; her New York club alone had 8,000 members. Some had signed up when *She Done Him Wrong* was first released in 1933, whereas others came on board in more recent years. Dolly Dempsey, the president of the original 1933 club, remained a loyal fan throughout West's life. In 1959, Walter Johnston, the president of the New York, New Jersey, and

Connecticut Mae West Club, which was formed in 1943, claimed 3,000 members. Accurate and reliable numbers cannot be determined, but one thing was certain: All of these fans were loyal to Miss West, as they called her.

West's long-time associate and friend, Jim Timony, died in April 1954, thereby ending a long relationship. The vacuum was filled by one of the musclemen in her act, Mr. California, Chester Ribonsky, who became her companion in what turned out to be a lifelong commitment. At West's behest, he changed his name to Chuck Krasner, and later to Paul Novak. He often accompanied her to movie premieres or parties. He acted as her prompter when she lost her train of thought during an interview and became her all-around manager. All observers commented on his great devotion. Although two generations divided them in age, they appeared quite compatible. West always gave the impression that she remained sexually active and interested and that her many musclemen played private roles in her life as well as public roles in her night club act.

Novak displayed his devotion to West in a highly public way on June 6, 1956, when he knocked out Mr. Universe, another performer in the act, in West's dressing room during a press conference. Novak claimed self-defense in court, but the Mr. Universe of 1956, Mickey Hargitay, insisted that Novak hit him because Mae West was jealous of Hargitay's romance with movie star Jayne Mansfield. Novak seemed to act in defense of West's image and feelings. All of the charges and countercharges received ample press coverage. As usual, the newspapers loved a Mae West story. They covered Novak's trial for assault and wrote in detail about West's appearances in court, her clothes, and her comments.

As the New York *Post* account observed: "An SRO audience which frequently broke into laughter during the testimony divided its attention between the muscle man and Miss West, who remained in court throughout, wearing dark glasses to shield her eyes from the indirect lighting." Hargitay left the night club act and later married Jayne Mansfield, who never lost an opportunity to snipe at West. Three years later, Mansfield told reporters she was sorry West's show had closed early in Las Vegas, to which West retorted: "That woman doesn't even exist as far as I'm concerned." West did not seem bothered by any publicity that got her name and picture in the papers.

But there was a level below which even she would not descend. It was reached when the exposé magazine of the 1950s, *Confidential,* published an article in November 1955 entitled "Mae West's Open Door Policy!" The article claimed that black boxer Chalky Wright had been West's live-in chauffeur in the mid-1930s, a position also held by other boxers, black, Hispanic, and white. West called the article "silly" and, two years later, when *Confidential* was being sued by other stars for libel and for publishing lewd material about them, Mae West offered to testify against the magazine. However, there were enough plaintiffs in the case that her testimony was not necessary. She claimed to have proof that repudiated their allegations about her.

The negative publicity associated with the Novak-Hargitay fight and the *Confidential* magazine article touched the seamier, messier, and racier sides of West's sexual exploits. Although she claimed continual interest in sexual variety and saw nothing un- usual about the fact that twenty-three-year-old men such as Novak preferred a sixty-three-year-old woman to a contempo- rary, she never acknowledged sexual jealousy and shrugged off any charges of power plays or possessiveness. She did not admit to any instances in which the men in her life took advantage of her. Her public persona only recognized her preeminence; she must always be in charge of the sexual game. Hargitay broke the rules of the image by beginning a very public romance with an- other sex goddess; he had to be removed, but unfortunately, it did not happen without the public fight between him and West's prime companion, Paul Novak.

The biracial theme exposed in *Confidential* was not a subject West wished to discuss publicly either. Although there had been whisperings since the 1920s that she enjoyed men of all colors as long as they were well-shaped, this subject was deemed too ex- plosive and too sensitive to receive public airing in the conserva- tive 1950s. Just as West enjoyed the company of homosexual men, who were among her most loyal fans, so she liked the company of boxers and wrestlers, black and white. She had always employed black actors and actresses; Louise Beavers, who had appeared in her movies, was in her night club act as well. But biracial friendships and biracial sexual relationships were two very different things. And although Mae West expressed audacity and independence on the subject of sex, she clammed up when it came to discussing her private sexual life.

Mae West's escapades during the 1950s received regular media exposure precisely because of her status as both a cult star and a celebrity. Her fans avidly followed her exploits in the racy gossip magazines as well as in the more mainstream press. Intellectuals who had paid attention to her briefly in the 1920s, resumed their interest in the 1960s, when her iconographic importance was indisputable. Although nonbelievers may have found her grasping for attention pathetic and embarassing, neither she nor her followers viewed her life and activities in this way. They admired the old war-horse for her spunk and her continued belief in herself. Mae West continued to grant interviews dressed in peignoirs, daring the reporter to find age lines on her flawless skin. The fact that interviews were still sought confirms her enduring status as a public figure.

West helped maintain her celebrity by writing her autobiography in the late 1950s. What better way to ensure that her version of her life story would be immortalized? West claimed that a fire had destroyed childhood pictures and letters and that she had to rely upon her memory, as well as that of her sister, Beverly, to reconstruct her early life. *Goodness Had Nothing to Do with It,* published in 1959, was a bestseller and gave her yet another opportunity to present herself in the most favorable light to her adoring public. The book described her smooth ride to the top and asserted that her uniqueness was the primary reason for her forty-year career.

Goodness Had Nothing to Do with It, by 1990s standards, is a rather tame account of West's personal and professional experiences. She refers to her lovers by their first names or no names at all: there are no explicit or graphic accounts of her sexual tastes or habits. Rather, there are mystical references to the ecstasy of love, punctuated by West's wry, sly humor. Readers were constantly reminded that West's first and only priority was herself. Toward the end of the book, for example, she reminded everyone that she always feared total love and involvement because it would detract from her primary interest: "This sense of spiritual union scared me. It could mean, if I let it, a too complete surrender—the surrender of personality I have always fought against. I have never wanted a love that meant absorption of my whole being, a surrender of my self-possession. A love like that is too all-consuming."

There is no discussion of frustrations, setbacks, or health problems. West portrays her difficulties with the censors throughout her Broadway and Hollywood career as minor inconveniences that she easily overcame. Indeed, all impediments are portrayed as useful aids on the path to her inevitable success. How she creates her image, how she knits together features she learned from other performers, are noticably absent from her account. But by 1959, Mae West was the primary and exclusive source on her life and her past—and most interviewers never challenged her version.

Reviewers gave the book a lot of attention. Although the Newark *Evening News* reviewer thought that West's descriptions of her love affairs were tasteless and boring, Arthur Mayer, Paramount's public relations man in the 1930s, enjoyed her reminiscences and thought she was "as competent with words as with wiggles." As usual, West's critical reception was mixed, but the audience loved her. The New York *Mirror* serialized portions of the book in October 1959 and the English press remained unabashed fans. As one London writer noted: "Small wonder that Miss West never had an understudy, as audiences went to the theatre for a Mae West performance and realized no other actress could give it them."

In the late 1950s, television discovered Mae West. This medium, which shared conservative values with the radio and movies, experimented with nostalgia and decided that Mae West would attract many viewers. The producers of the televised 1958 Academy Award presentations paired the old sex comic with movie heartthrob Rock Hudson. They sang "Baby, It's Cold Outside" and the audience response was enthusiastic. West supplied her own lyrics and brought down the house with her good-natured and predictable spoof on love and romance. This appearance introduced Mae West to members of the younger generation. She told columnist Earl Wilson that her two-minute appearance was so popular that it had been "bootlegged in Italy and other places."

Television had first entered American homes in the late 1940s, and by the time of West's first appearance, it was quickly becoming the dominant medium of entertainment and information for all Americans. Whether the ever-present censors would find the sixty-six-year-old star objectionable or not remained to be seen. In 1956, she had told an interviewer that TV was "tryin' to cramp my style. Why, they practically want to put me in a Mother Hubbard dress and dark glasses." West seemed wary of the new medium, much like her skeptical approach to Hollywood in the early 1930s.

But after her successful appearance on the Academy Award Show and the willingness of other producers to invite her on, she decided, in May 1959, to appear on Dean Martin's show along with Bob Hope. Martin was quoted as saying: "I hope she keeps it clean because I want to be on some more." The hope or fear of controversy did not materialize. West used many of her old lines, such as "Come up and see me some time," and "peel me a grape," to the delight of the studio audience. She sang/talked her way through "I Can't Give You Anything but Love" and admitted that she did not own a television set. TV critic Harriet Van Horne reviewed West's appearance favorably: "Her act is not family entertainment, to be sure. But her vulgarity is so monstrous, so unabashed, that it's a sublime parody on all the sirens and courtesans and shady ladies who ever lived." Whether it was West's presence or the popular Bob

Hope's, or both, the show had almost double the ratings of the Ed Sullivan Show, a staple of Sunday night television in those days.

Each television network had its own censor. Because the air waves were publicly mandated, although they were used for private profit, television executives were ever mindful of public taste, and were careful never to offend viewers, who would then boycott their shows, refuse to buy the advertised products, and bring doom to the network. Mae West, at age sixty-six, was still considered a threat to American sensibilities. Her humorous approach to the most controversial subject in the country was lost on the fearful. The fact that censors still existed and still considered her offensive suggests that Americans' attitudes on discussions of sex remained problematical in the 1960s.

West's next scheduled television appearance fulfilled the censors' fears. CBS announced that Mae West was to be interviewed on the prestigious "Person to Person" show by Charles Collingwood, a distinguished reporter. (Collingwood had replaced the legendary Edward R. Murrow that year as host of the show.) The interview was to air on October 16, 1959. Instead of filming the interview before an audience, the usual procedure, CBS had videotaped it, a new process for television, in West's apartment on October 4th. Apparently the network executives did not trust West and wanted to preview her appearance. They clearly did not like what they saw. The day before the scheduled airing, CBS released a terse announcement cancelling the show: "In the opinion of the network, it was felt that certain portions of the interview with Mae West might be misconstrued." West was reached by telephone in San Francisco and told a reporter: "I don't know what they could have misconstrued. Certain minds always misconstrue everything. I have a very big public that understands what I say." She added that she had only agreed to the interview in order to publicize her autobiography. "I was asked questions from my autobiography, which is honest and frank and deals with sex all the way through the book." She acknowledged to the reporter that the CBS cameraman filmed a nude statue of her that stood in her living room as well as her very famous bedroom with mirrors all around and a canopied bed. "But I did wear a very sedate, dignified gown."

West's nonappearance on "Person to Person" gave her more publicity than if she had appeared. Collingwood was quoted as saying: "She has been doing her show for half a century. I didn't find it offensive, or I wouldn't have done it." All of the big-city newspapers picked up the story, and some reporters who had been treated to a preview of the interview told other reporters their impressions. The *Variety* reporter, who had been among the privileged few to view the videotape, published his notes in *Variety* a few days later. Among the vintage West lines that probably offended the CBS executives was her answer to Collingwood's question: "Are you interested in current problems like foreign affairs?" West's reply: "Oh, I've always had a weakness for foreign affairs. See Chapter Five and I believe Chapter Nine in the book." When asked what she thought about the new space age, she said: "A man in space is a waste—the man, I mean, not the idea."

In other words, it was typical Mae West. Yet in October 1959 television executives and their anxious censors who represented the advertisers decided to play it safe and cancel the show. In concluding the interview, Collingwood asked her how it felt to be an American institution. She answered: "Oh, wonderful— and I've got the constitution to prove it." Obviously, the CBS executives did not regard her as an American institution and they did not consider her constitution worthy of display on their venerable network. A sense of humor was clearly not a prerequisite for executive status in television. The 1959 cancellation of West's TV appearance suggested that America was not yet mature, sophisticated, tolerant, or relaxed enough to withstand a few minutes with a sixty-six-year-old sex goddess.

The inconsistency and unpredictability of TV executives, however, dictated that a few months later the very same network would allow West to appear on March 1, 1960, on the popular comedy program, the "Red Skelton Show." There was no public explanation for this about-face. Perhaps the entertainment division of the network could handle her wit better than the news division. In any event, West spoofed the "Person to Person" show with a skit called "Meet the Author," in which Skelton played the interviewer as well as many of the men in her life. West had the opportunity to publicize her book and to remind her fans that she was still around. She sang "It's So Nice to Have a Man Around the House," and "I May Add an Extra Fellow Here and There" to which the male chorus responded: "The more the better."

It would be four years before she returned to the little screen. In 1964, she made two appearances on the popular comedy show "Mr. Ed," which starred a talking horse. West's predictable style and her advancing age made her an unlikely regular on television. Further, it would have to be an adventurous producer who sought her talents. Clearly the producer of "Mr. Ed" fit the bill. When she appeared, in March 1964, on the show, one television reporter noted: "Mae was treated like visiting royalty. When she came out of her dressing room, she was approached for autographs; when she went before the cameras the usual sideline conversation on the set ceased." By this point, she was often viewed as a curiosity as much as a living, breathing star. The director of "Mr. Ed," Arthur Lubin, had been a young production assistant on *She Done Him Wrong* back in 1933 and he was clearly delighted to greet his one-time idol. West acknowledged that "Mr. Ed's" audience—children—was not her usual one, but she continued: "You know, I now have three generations of fans and there are lots of new fan clubs among teenagers." She also told the interviewer that young people had seen her on the Academy Awards telecast. "I got fan mail for two years after that. And they see some of my old pictures on 'The Late Show.'"

Though her energy level was not what it used to be, and she often walked in a stilted manner and forgot some of her lines, West continued to perform. At sixty-eight, she returned to live theater. Beginning in the spring of 1961, she toured the country with a play of her own creation, *Sextette*. This flimsy offering re-volved around the question of whether West's character's sixth husband would enjoy his honeymoon without interruption. The major activity in the play was the surprise appearance of each of her previous five husbands, none of whom had been known to number six. As usual, the audiences loved it. At the Coconut Grove Playhouse in Miami, West received a two-minute ovation as she entered the stage. In Chicago, at the Edgewater Beach Playhouse, the crowds stayed on after the performance to ap-plaud her some more. "She is a trouper of the old order," stated one critic. "Time has failed to dim her uncanny sense of tim-ing," said Helen Muir in the Miami *News,* and Paul Bruun wrote: "Throughout the evening, I heard lavish adjectives of praise for Mae West and for this play."

"Still Going Strong at Seventy" was the headline for another account of her 1961 performance, although West was only admit-ting to sixty-eight years at that time. But the vigor and bravado, although still evident, became harder to produce. In 1964, not long after her television appearances on "Mr. Ed," she was hos-pitalized, first for diabetes, and then with a mild heart attack. Her well-publicized devotion to proper diet and exercise could not stave off the aging process forever. Her occasional indul-gence in sweets now had to be restricted, a task handled by the ever faithful Paul Novak. As Harriet Van Horne had said of her appearance on the Dean Martin Show: "She's a gallant old girl . . . most noticeable change is in the famous hour-glass figure. Mae still shakes a sexy shoulder and gyrates her hips with deadly inflection, but it's a bit difficult to project sinful abandon when one is corseted as firmly as a broken limb."

Miraculously, or perhaps just fortuitously, Mae West's end-less interest in public display, her high self-esteem, and her con-fident belief that new generations of fans were waiting for her to appear enabled the Baby Boom generation of the mid-1960s to experience the West phenomenon. So many of the themes that she had been exploiting for years became fashionable during that decade. Sexual liberation, women's liberation, gay liberation—all ideas and movements that gained currency in the period, and often shocked the society's elders, seemed to be old hat to West, whose turn it was to wonder what the fuss was all about. Mae West was made for the modern era; she knew it and her fans, the old and new ones, enthusiastically agreed.

All of West's one-liners took on new meaning and power in the 1960s. In 1967, a collection of her words was published as *The Wit and Wisdom of Mae West*. Late-time television featured her old movies, and rerun movie houses held Mae West festivals. Her style, as a no-nonsense woman, evoked positive responses from the teenagers and college students who considered rebellion a virtue. Almost inadvertently, Mae West found herself a vital force among young people as she moved through old age. Her vanity and her ego kept her heavily made up and before the public. While some observers saw her as a caricature of herself, most continued to admire her spunk and her wit.

CHAPTER FIVE

Be Cool and Collect

1965–1980 AND BEYOND

Although West's performances were limited after 1965, they were not over. Despite her great self-confidence, her failing health prevented frequent public appearances. However, the applause of a live audience, the crowds seeking a glimpse of the celebrity, and the extensive press coverage remained as necessary to Mae West as daily walks and fan mail. The many interviewers who came to the Ravenswood Hotel to see the aging star in her apartment (with its 1930s decor still intact) marveled over her regal appearance and her serious assumption that the visitor was lucky indeed to meet her. She prided herself on being interested in current musical trends, although she could not claim equal interest in contemporary political affairs. She received an invitation to dinner at the White House from President Lyndon B. Johnson, but she refused it. The trip to Washington would have been too taxing. Rock 'n' roll intrigued her and she made a record album in the mid-1960s in which she sang, in a surprisingly strong and vibrant voice, rock classics such as "Twist and Shout." The album had moderate sales.

When an overzealous interviewer in 1970 asked her questions about Vietnam and women's liberation, her answers ranged from predictable to unpredictable. On women's liberation: "I'm all for it. All the way. Gentlemen prefer blondes. But who says blondes prefer gentlemen?'' On gay liberation: "The gay boys? Looks like they're takin' over, doesn't it? They're crazy about me. I'm so flamboyant.''

But when asked about the longest war in American history, she began: "I hate wars. I'm against all wars.'' This safe response, however, was followed by a list of social complaints in which she suggested that student unrest, division over the war, and differences between conservatives and radicals were inspired by a conspiracy. It was unclear who the conspirators were. When questioned further, she continued: "Communists have done a lot of good things. You can't tear them down. They're the ones who got old-age pensions, money for the poor, unemployment so they can at least live.'' At this point, the 20th-Century Fox publicity man, who had arranged the interview, began making choking sounds and concluded. "She means socialism, not communism.'' According to the report, West nodded in agreement. In 1970, the Cold War mentality still prevailed and no one, surely not an old bawdy woman star, should say anything positive about the Soviet system of government. Richard Nixon's policy of detente had not yet emerged and Hollywood, ever sensitive to public opinion, would not dream of going out on a limb politically. Mae West, of course, knew little about geopolitics or the Cold War; the apolitical entertainer simply uttered what, to her, were commonsensical views on the human condition and in favor of systems that spoke for the downtrodden.

Throughout the 1960s and 1970s, Mae West faced reporters who were accustomed to asking famous people questions about current events, world issues, and anything else that occurred to them. Earlier generations of journalists had never asked popular culture stars their opinions on anything. The only time entertainers showed concern for political events was during wartime, when they demonstrated their patriotism by singing or appearing on stage during campaigns to sell war bonds. By the late 1960s, however, with the omnipresence of television, and with the growth of a mass audience interested in their favorite star's every thought and action, reporters began to ask pertinent, impertinent, and seemingly irrelevant questions of stars.

As evidence of West's celebrity status, such prestigious newspapers as the *New York Times* wrote long feature articles about her. Steven V. Roberts, in a 1969 piece, called her a "pop poster." He asserted that, like W. C. Fields and Humphrey Bogart, "she had a flip insolence and self-assurance that appeals to an iconoclastic generation." According to this analysis, West was unchanging, while the contemporary youth had become "iconoclastic," in contrast to the conformity of the 1950s' generation. These generalizations typified the critics' efforts to explain her continued popularity. Newspaper and magazine readers seemed genuinely interested in the opinions of the aging bawdy entertainer.

Among her rare public appearances in the later years of her life were those at the awards banquet of Delta Kappa Alpha, the cinema fraternity at the University of Southern California. Mae West first appeared at the event in 1967 and received a standing ovation. She answered questions while reclining on a chaise lounge on stage. Her appearance was so well received that she came back the following year and again in 1970. Reporters commented on how the blasé Hollywood audience, filled with stars, became fans in West's presence. And she took it all in as her due. One Hollywood writer noted "her professional ability to remain a star, despite inactivity, even in the sometimes jaded, cynical, what-have-you-done-lately atmosphere of Hollywood." Her youthful appearance always received attention, as did how much the audience enjoyed the old lines yet again. When West thanked the men in the audience for their "heavy breathing," a line she had been using for fifty years, the audience laughed. In May 1971, the UCLA student body voted her the "Woman of the Century" and showed her film *I'm No Angel*. West appeared afterwards to answer questions.

Throughout the 1930s, when West was making movies, she did not receive the recognition or respect of the Hollywood community. She insisted that she was not interested in socializing with the stars, but it seems that they were not interested in her, either. By the late 1960s, however, a new generation of actors, curious and fascinated by the old-time legends in their midst, began to honor them, the last living reminders of the Golden Age of Hollywood. The reclusive Garbo was photographed every time she left her New York City apartment; feminists discovered Katharine Hepburn and Bette Davis; and both young stars and film buffs honored male and female survivors of the 1930s. Hollywood showed a renewed interest in its own past and within that framework, Mae West emerged as one of the most popular stars to receive recognition.

College youth in the 1960s displayed a wide range of behavior. While some demonstrated against the war in Vietnam, others held fraternity celebrations featuring old movie stars. Some activists insisted upon tearing down all traditions while other students enjoyed nostalgia. The spectrum of values and actions was wide, and for the group who admired old movies and outrageously dressed women stars, Mae West was the last word. Her persistent belief in her self worth contributed, not only to her image, but to the ideology of the period. Self-centered individualism became a key feature in the value system of many youth and Mae West sounded like an appropriate representative.

The greatest splash she made during the final years, however, was in July 1970 when the film *Myra Breckinridge* premiered in New York City. West played a talent agent in this X-rated satire of Hollywood. Based upon the Gore Vidal novel, the movie proved to be a tasteless treatment; some of West's more crude scenes were cut out of the final screen version. By this time, Hollywood had developed a ratings system as a compromise between the advocates of censorship and the liberals who wanted no restrictions at all. By rating a film, with an X mandating adults-only attendance, the traditionalists were satisfied. In the case of *Myra Breckinridge,* it assured lots of publicity. West was paid $350,000 for her brief appearance in the movie, a reminder of her continuing financial power.

Though the current sex queen, Raquel Welch, starred in the film, 20th-Century Fox, the movie's producer, wisely trumpeted Mae West's appearance at the premiere. (The news reports erroneously said that it had been twenty years since she had been in New York; it actually had been fourteen.) The wire services carried the news of her visit, as did all of the New York papers. The story was on the front page of the San Francisco *Examiner* and page eight of the Los Angeles *Times*. Thousands crammed the streets around the theater to get a peek at her; millions of others read about her in their morning paper. She held a press conference the day after the premiere in which 200 members of the world press sat in the night club of the Americana Hotel and heard her deliver her usual lines: "You got to be healthy in order to be sexy," and "yes, I discovered Cary Grant."

The 1970 trip to New York was also notable because West traveled by airplane for the first time. She took it in stride, accompanied by Paul Novak, a maid, and the studio entourage. She maintained her public persona as a queen deigning to appear before her adoring public. And, much to the fascination of the writers, the audience obliged by behaving like adoring subjects. Among the members of the premiere audience was "wild and wooly Janis Joplin," noted one account. Joplin, a well-known rock 'n' roller, was accompanied by another rock singer, Johnny Winter, "whose long, white-blonde locks caused balcony sitters to applaud, thinking he was Miss West," wrote Addison Verrill in *Variety*. The liberated Mae West found kindred spirits among the rock crowd as well as the young feminists. They all loved her single-minded devotion to personal pleasure as well as her willingness at age seventy-seven to talk about sex.

This highly publicized appearance gave rise to yet more analyses of "What Makes Mae West Endure." The answers varied, of course, but many pointed to her comedic talent. Magazine writer Deac Rossell said she was "primally funny" and "her own best parodist," and another writer brought out Will Rogers's remark in the 1930s that she was "the most interesting woman in Hollywood." Chauncey Howell covered the press conference the next day and noted the "wire service girls with Fem Lib buttons where their circle pins used to quiver at Smith." Amazed at her virtuoso performance, most of the young women present let out an audible "Wow" when West left and swore to give up smoking if they could look like her at seventy-seven. When one interviewer asked West why she made a comeback in *Myra,* she retorted: "...it's not a comeback, I've never been away, never stopped."

"The women loved her," wrote Barbara Long in *The Village Voice,* "because she posed no threat now, and, as a parody of sexuality, never had." West's high wages for her small part in *Myra Breckinridge* reminded writers of her financial astuteness and that she had extensive holdings in the San Fernando Valley; Frank Taylor, in the *Newark Evening News,* quoted wags who said: "two people own the San Fernando Valley: Mae West and Bob Hope." Some recalled that she had been the highest paid actress in the depression years. Others continued to marvel at her youthful appearance. In short, few talked about the movie role, but focused instead on West's inimitable personality and philosophy. After the flurry of publicity surrounding *Myra,* writers dutifully reported her latest projects, most of which never came to fruition. Her television appearance on a Dick Cavett special in April 1976 received a lot of attention, with critics praising her but generally panning the show. John J. O'Connor, the *New York Times* television critic, said: "She is something—a wonderful, glamorous, talented and marvelously witty something—unto herself." She told one interviewer that she did not want to do too much television because: "I don't want 'em to see me for nothing." But she quickly added that she had no plans to retire. "If you like what you are doing, like me, never, never retire."

In 1977, when West made *Sextette,* a tired movie based upon old material of hers, she was eighty-four years old and still actively interested in public performance. *Sextette* came out in 1978, and was described by Vincent Canby in the *New York Times* as "a disorienting freak show." Although the film promoters had difficulties finding a distributor and few people paid the admission price to see the film, the critics, as usual, took notice. One reporter wrote: "The extreme fascination of *Sextette* derives not merely from its star's age...but from the fact that the film pretends not to notice it." Others commented on her awkward movements and seeming inability to remember her inane lines. Nevertheless, the very fact that Mae West was still alive and performing astonished many. According to Dom De Luise, one of her costars in the movie, "she never looked a day over fifty, and, on good days, she looked forty." Although the film's cast included Timothy Dalton and Tony Curtis, with guest appearances by gossip columnist Rona Barrett and sports broadcaster Howard Cosell, *Sextette* died quietly but quickly.

West granted a few interviews in her last years, offering the same stories to new writers; because the reporters rarely did their homework, they assumed that her words were fresh and meant for them alone. If they had read the clipping files for the previous thirty years, they would have noted the same questions and answers recorded many times in the past. In August 1980, West suffered a stroke. That well-kept body of which she was so very proud was, after all, mortal. The president of her original fan club, Dolly Dempsey, came up from San Diego to help take care of her. Mae West died on November 22, 1980. She was eighty-seven years old.

Mae West's continuous activity contributed to her image and fame. Because she never retired and used the press's interest in her so successfully, she remained in the public eye for three generations. Ironically, her image, of course, did not change substantially over the years since its formation as Diamond Lil in 1928. Although other popular culture figures tried to stay current by making themselves over to accommodate a fickle audience, West acted as though Lil's allure was eternal. She believed that there was no need to change perfection; her parody of sex played to all ages and all audiences. Time confirmed the correctness of this belief. Children and grandchildren of her original fans continued to go to her shows and movies to see the legend.

Although the Mae West image was clearly delineated, she allowed a variety of interpretations of its meaning. If women's liberation advocates saw Mae West/Diamond Lil as a kindred spirit, fine; if gay rights advocates embraced her as one of them, so be it. If advocates of free speech praised her highminded stand against censorship in the 1920s and 1930s, she agreed with them. If asked in the 1960s or 1970s whether she approved of nudity on the screen, however, she answered no. Leave something to the imagination, she advised, as she had always done herself. Her prophetic ability or her good fortune (or both) to anticipate some of the enduring themes of the twentieth century assured her a place in popular culture.

Late-night television, in need of material, began to run old movies in the 1960s. This proved a gold mine for the old studios as well as an opportunity for the stars of earlier years to gain a new audience. The fact that Mae West continued to make appearances while *She Done Him Wrong* attracted new fans only increased her celebrity status. The fact that she had been a life-long health advocate in a period when jogging and diets became a national preoccupation contributed further to her image. People were beginning to live longer lives, and in the 1970s experts were beginning to acknowledge that older people continued to have sex lives. Gerontology, a growing discipline engaged in the formal study of aging, made Mae West seem to be a living marvel.

Mae West can also be viewed as the American Eve *and* Adam. She was not only the personification of the sexual temptress telling innocent men (Adams) to come up and see her some time, but she was Adam as well—a union of traits that produced not a hermaphrodite but the first person. She developed her own identity from scratch, or at least from a careful shaping of traits developed on the vaudeville stage. As literary historian R. W. B. Lewis has shown, this country has a long tradition of male heroes who create themselves. Mae West entered that maledominated tradition and left her background and her predetermined culture to create her own personality. She captured the American desire for freedom, independence, and self-determination. In this way, she could appeal to men and women. As writer Barbara Long had suggested, she posed no threat to women because she offered them the humorous opportunity to satirize everyone's preoccupation with sex at the same time that she gave the women in her audience the vision of an independent woman.

Mae West's singular focus upon sexuality became her trademark throughout the century. Just as Susan B. Anthony will always be remembered as a major suffrage leader and Jane Addams is associated with the settlement house movement, so Mae West emerges throughout the twentieth century as a popular culture heroine who stood for women's freedom, sexual honesty, the right to find one's own identity, and freedom of expression. The fact that she was apolitical, and never associated with any social movement of the day, contributed to her longevity. She supported no one political party or one reform effort. She stood for individualism in a society that treasured that quality; all peoples, of all persuasions, could glean positive messages from her image. The movies gave her her largest audience, but word of mouth formed the foundation of her fame. Her live appearances, from vaudeville to night clubs, built a solid base of fans. Television reruns introduced her movies to the younger generation.

The importance of her sense of humor cannot be underestimated. Americans, like all people, love to laugh. Mae West made them laugh through the Great War, the depression, World War II, Korea, and Vietnam. The subject matter of her humor, of course, only accentuated the laugh. To kid about the forbidden subject defied all cultural expectations. For a woman to laugh about a most unladylike subject added more fuel to the fire. To continue to preach the same message when she was in her fifties, sixties, and seventies, thereby defying another cultural assumption, accentuated her idiosyncratic status. Older people, especially older women, were not supposed to be interested in sex. By the 1960s, when various reform movements took shape, including such organized advocates for the elderly as the Gray Panthers, Mae West found that she had inadvertently supported another cause.

Mae West, as the most famous example of the bawdy woman performer, helped transform woman's role in America by transgressing it. She challenged society's values about women in the boldest way possible. This was the source of her humor and her power. Because she had such constant exposure, she reinforced the image of the take-charge woman for her growing audience. Certainly many people of all ages had heard enough about Mae West to associate her with bawdiness, and in so doing, they beheld a view of women unlike the traditional one. Surely most women did not want to look like, or behave like, Mae West, but they may have secretly admired her freedom, influence, and power. They surely applauded her financial freedom, her ability to speak her mind freely, and her opportunity to shape her life according to her own desires. Her male fans may not have wanted their wives to be as outspoken and independent as Mae West, but they surely enjoyed her easy camaraderie, her good-naturedness, and her willingness to engage in both sexual discussions and sexual play.

Mae West's regular commentaries on marriage, family, and children also received public notice. West was never bashful about telling the interviewer that she never regretted not having children; she also admitted that the one short-lived marriage of her youth was a mistake. West never preached or told other women what to do, but she spoke in a forthright manner about her life choices and appeared very contented with them. She separated the sexually interested woman from the prostitute, expressing sympathy for the woman who had to use her body for financial return. She offered American men and women a very different view of sexuality, one in which both sexes could enjoy the natural act without anxiety or guilt; above all, without guilt.

Paradoxically, Mae West never declared war on women's roles in America. Rather, she undermined them by her very being. She did not use the reformer's tactic of a frontal assault, but poked fun at the prudishness and the hypocrisy that she saw all around her. The very men who came to see her play *Sex* in New

York City acted self-righteous and declared her actions immoral when asked about them. Mae West, the undeclared feminist, upheld one of feminism's most sacred principles: the belief in woman's equality. Just as men have the right to sexual experience and pleasure, she felt, so do women; to West, this appeared obvious, commonsensical, and just.

From a 1990s perspective, Mae West seems to have, unconsciously perhaps, deconstructed the society's image of sexuality. That is to say, she broke down cultural attitudes about sex and rebuilt them, with women playing dominant and initiating roles. According to traditional views, men play the determining and dominating role in sexual matters; they initiate the encounter and they propose dates, engagements, and marriage to their female partners. Women, traditionally demure and passive, are to wait for the male initiative. This viewpoint, of course, was publicly challenged in the 1960s, but when Mae West began her career in the early years of this century, the traditional position was supreme. West's behavior on the stage challenged the customary image of woman as sexually passive. She showed that women were interested in sex, had sexual desires, and wanted to control that aspect of their lives. As West said on many occasions, she was interested in the life in her men, not the men in her life. Also, *she* could do *him* wrong, but she would not tolerate the age-old pattern of the man doing the woman wrong.

According to leftist critics, marriage had been invented by men to ensure the faithfulness of their wives, whereas the so-called double standard allowed married men to roam. Mae West confronted this view and laughed at it. She was always interested in multiple partners, she claimed, and saw nothing immoral or outrageous in her taste. She had a large sexual appetite, she said, just like many men and, she suspected, many women as well. If you were not married, why not indulge? West drew the line at married lovers. But she believed that not all women were destined for marriage, and if she could find single men with whom she could enjoy life, that was wonderful. At this level, her humorously presented critique of accepted practices became truly revolutionary. Marriage and family remain the bedrock of American culture. The number of people living their adult lives as singles did not become statistically significant until the 1970s. Again, Mae West anticipated social trends.

If 1960s youth found Mae West appealing, the narcissistic "Me generation" of the 1970s must have worshipped her. After all, West lived for herself and she was not ashamed to admit it. Her life's work was cherishing herself and preserving her body and her reputation. It was a full-time occupation and a very pleasant preoccupation. West abandoned the carefully nourished ideal of the woman who was self-sacrificing in favor of the individualistic goal of personal happiness. Rugged, individualistic America had always heralded male examples of independence and even ruthlessness, but did not applaud the concept in women. Mae West offered women an audacious example of a woman successfully thinking of herself first. What appeared as funny or outrageous to earlier generations became the watchword of the 1970s and 1980s.

A careful analysis of West's egocentrism provides a revealing glimpse of our culture's values. The shock of hearing a woman renounce marriage and motherhood in favor of self-development and self-satisfaction made the listener laugh uncomfortably. A man who announced similar wishes would be accepted without comment. Surely women missed the opportunity in earlier generations to examine the meaning of personal happiness at the expense of family and community. Mae West's self-preoccupation was so extreme and exaggerated as to seem almost harmless. No one else could be as totally devoted to self as she was.

In earlier times, social critics attacked Mae West's unconventional views on women's sexuality. In the 1970s and 1980s, conservatives ignored her. If they chose to use her as a symbol of the total self absorption of the current generation, they may have found interested listeners. Mae West's views were subversive. She believed that she was the total universe. As she told C. Robert Jennings in a *Playboy* interview in 1971, "I'm my own original creation." She described herself as "a forceful, dominatin' sex personality that requires multiple men, like I always had in real life." She told Richard Merman, in a 1969 *Life* interview: "I always figured, never leave yourself down to one man or one dollar."

"I see myself as a classic. I never loved another person the way I loved myself. I've had an easy life and no guilts about it." The directness, simplicity, and boldness of these sentences struck readers as ingenuous, funny, and possibly strange. But overall, the impression was positive and just contributed to continued curiosity about the living legend. Only Mae West, who in 1971 was seventy-eight years old and still not counting, had the nerve to declare such an attitude publicly. When asked whether she ever tired of sustaining that "larger-than-life erotic image," she replied: "You can't get enough of a good thing, in my opinion."

Mae West was perfectly serious when she compared herself to the great dramatic actress Sarah Bernhardt. She regarded herself as a dramatic as well as a comedic actress. She rarely acknowledged anyone else who could compare with her. "Well, I always said Chaplin was the only other person who could write his own pictures and star in 'em, too," she told Jennings in the *Playboy* interview. Interviewers wondered whether or not she believed her self-aggrandizing claims; most concluded that she was perfectly serious. The bragging woman was yet another atypical pose for American women; most displayed modesty in their descriptions of themselves. Few proclaimed their strength, beauty, or wit for all to hear; few, of course, qualified, according to West. When she met the reclusive Greta Garbo in the 1960s, according to her account, she wondered what they would talk about, but quickly resolved the dilemma by talking about herself the whole time they were together, a subject that she assumed interested Garbo.

Mae West's vigorous individualism denied anyone else's existence. If her philosophy had been adopted by large numbers of women, there would be no future generation. Because she was rich and famous, she was able to indulge all of her needs and surround herself with admirers who acted as family members. She possessed the material rewards that this culture provides for its successful members and seemingly lived a very satisfying life. She chose a public life rather than a private one and by all accounts, had no regrets.

Mae West shrewdly told Bob Thomas, one of her favorite reporters (who was also a fan, as were most of the people who wrote about her), in 1973: "Sex is like a small business; you gotta watch over it." West understood that nourishing your most profitable asset was good business practice. She also enjoyed giving advice on personal habits and beliefs. She found it perfectly natural that reporters sought her wise words on ways to live. The health-conscious 1970s seemed made for West's philosophy. She wrote a book in 1973, "My Guide to Looking Young," in which she said: "I never worry. Worry kills you, ruins your health and nervous system. I don't think negative thoughts."

The how-to audience read the words of an experienced and successful practitioner of her own system. "Never think more of someone else than you do of yourself," she counseled. She shared her exercise regimen as well as her daily schedule. The youth-conscious American, particularly the Californian, looked in admiration at pictures of the eighty-year-old actress. In fact, the 1970s generation merely caught up with Mae West; she had been practicing her principles of self-absorption, youthfulness, and physical and mental fitness for sixty years.

In 1975, West acknowledged that she was not a reader and that she used her experiences with men to obtain ideas for her plays. Her skimpy elementary school education and her many years on the road had prevented her from developing reading skills and habits. "I was never interested in women. I don't think I've had two girlfriends in my whole life. I never cared a thing about politics, or music, or traveling, or parties, or reading. I'm too nervous to read much." This admission was one of the rare glimpses of weakness in the otherwise perfect persona of Mae West. Even so, she interpreted it positively: nervousness, she observed, made her more active, more of a doer than a thinker about life. Her reliance upon men for both sexual pleasure and intellectual stimulation offered another example of role reversal: although men have used women sexually, they have relied on other men for their inspiration. Women have rarely been the users and exploiters of men, either sexually or intellectually.

Nervousness was not a characteristic usually identified with Mae West. Her peripatetic nature seemed tied to boundless energy and all-consuming ambition. But perhaps West experienced doubts and insecurities that resulted in nervous energy. Because she so rarely discussed this nervousness, it is hard to evaluate. Her lack of interest in reading, however, has been attributed to her overwhelming ego and her belief that she could write better material for herself than anyone else. After all, what else was reading for but to discover new properties in which to perform?

One of her last interviews was granted to Ellis Nassour for *Club* magazine in 1979. Making a grand entrance, as she always did, she greeted the reporter with her usual "Hiya." Nassour noted: "She smiles widely to assure you the teeth are all hers." With Paul Novak at her side, she was the perfect hostess. Nassour's assessment of her face viewed at close range was not flattering: "The face is pasty. She wears far too much makeup and it is badly and unevenly applied. The false eyelashes are a bit much and the wig is quite awful. . . ." Nassour was the first reporter to point out what must have been obvious to many other writers; the others, however, diplomatically preserved her aura by omitting these embarrassing facts. In most of the Nassour interview, though, West sounded like her usual self and gave him little to criticize. She reminded Nassour: "I still only play leads!" and she remained coy about her actual age. She admitted to having been born "Near the end of the nineteenth century." Whenever she wished to be another character or have a new experience, she wrote a script on the subject that she could star in. "I am not just a woman, but a star, a writer, and a thinker as well." When asked what makes a legend, she replied:

"The public made me. They responded to me since I was a child. I had something they liked. I gave them what they wanted."

Later in the interview, she talked about Elvis Presley, whom she liked, and said she thought "he [was] takin' what I did and settin' it to music." Just as she had introduced the suggestive shimmy shawabble to white audiences in vaudeville, so Presley swiveled his hips and "like me, he brought freedom and independence to the public." West also assured Nassour that she liked being a legend, unlike some stars. In an unusual deviation from her normal stance, she said that she was surprised by her success: "It just happened." (This uncharacteristic remark sounds like an old lady's response to a question asked one too many times.) She admitted to having a natural rapport with audiences and said that she believed that her constant activity contributed to her sharp mind and her ability to satisfy her fans. "I never stop. I'm always working on a project of some kind."

On the subject of sex, West said that people often said that she had invented it, but she hadn't; she just knew how to enjoy it. "I never felt I was a sinner. Sex is natural. I always believed in it. What comes naturally is not nasty." The women's liberation movement of the 1970s, West agreed, was good, but in her case: "I was born liberated!" Women should have equal opportunities, she continued, "but I don't believe a woman should try to replace love with a career. At the same time, we shouldn't sacrifice too much for a man.... No, I never wanted children... but I was my own baby." In conclusion, she told her interviewer: "Experience is by far the best teacher. You know, ever since I was a little girl I knew that if you look both ways when you cross the street, you'll see a lot more than traffic."

Charlotte Chandler interviewed Mae West in the last year of her life, 1980, and evoked some novel answers from the much-interviewed woman. Chandler asked West which was more important to her—sex or work. West's answer was a variation on her familiar theme: "For Lil, happiness was sex. For Mae, it was work." This separation of the Diamond Lil character from the real Mae West marked a change from previous remarks on this subject. Rather than declare the sameness of the image and the person, West finally assumed a critical distance from her most famous creation. West modified her claim that work was more important to her than sex by hastily adding that she needed sex to live as well. "As a child I had perfect confidence," she assured Chandler. "Men's thoughts and ambitions were like mine." Finally, "The real security is yourself." The self-centered Mae West never deviated from her essential egocentrism, and the 1980s generation found it as appealing as earlier ones had.

Chandler's interview (which became part of a larger book project) was excerpted in *Ms.* magazine in 1984, four years after West's death. It was both ironic and appropriate that the feminist popular journal of the period should print the interview and help to preserve the legendary status of a sex symbol. Her words were the last ones on her life and beliefs and provided the basis for all future evaluations. In one of her many obituaries, James McCourt recalled one of her best lines to sum up her life's work: "I invented myself, and I never put up with sloppy work." Mae West had the final interpretation of herself.

Imitation is said to be the highest form of flattery, and Mae West had many imitators. During her long life, gay entertainers often did impressions of her, strutting across the stage, uttering her lines, and wiggling their hips. West's flamboyance, which she often referred to herself, appealed to the gay community; along with Marlene Dietrich and Bette Davis, Mae West was a favorite subject of female impersonators. As gay liberation joined all of the other liberation movements in the late 1960s and 1970s, the gay community could publicly acknowledge its admiration for a woman they had long adored privately. West's treatment of homosexuals in her early plays, such as *The Drag,* gave her status in the gay community; they knew of her sympathy for them. In the 1970s, West looked like a prophet, whereas she saw herself as a no-nonsense observer of all sides of life, seamy, respectable, and in-between. The forbidden, in West's value system, did not exist. Her attraction to gays was based on a libertarian view of freedom, rather than a sense of human rights. When questioned about homosexuality, West expressed understanding and sympathy, but not advocacy. She believed that male homosexuals were women hidden in men's bodies and therefore to be treated with understanding. She benefited by her seeming support for a community and lifestyle that had little public support. And when the eighty-plus-year-old woman agreed with reporters that, yes, the gays had always liked her, she appeared to be as liberated in the 1970s as she had been in the 1920s.

Bette Midler, an entertainer who achieved stardom in the 1970s, incorporated much of the West style and dash into her very successful concert routine. "The Divine Miss M," who went on to become a major movie comic in the mid-to-late 1980s, began as a singer. Midler's songs and numbers were reminiscent of many of the great bawdy women singer-comics of an earlier era. Traces of West, Eva Tanguay, and Sophie Tucker could be detected in her often hilarious numbers. Midler's dialogues with the audience between her singing numbers used double entendres (as well as frank expressions), much as Mae West did. Midler's first success came in a New York gay bathhouse. Her constant references to sex, albeit bolder than West's, tied her to the earlier entertainer as well. Bette Midler stroked her body, just as Mae West did, and she admired herself, saying: "I am a living work of art." Both women declared their worth to their audiences as they strutted around the stage. Midler displayed the same bawdy humor; the primary difference was that her audience from the beginning consisted of both men and women, who laughed equally at her outrageous behavior.

West's songs, both in her vaudeville act and in her movies, always reminded the audience of what she had on her mind. Midler, reflecting a bolder time period, and the uninhibited, uncensored setting of a large concert hall, sometimes dispensed with the double entendres and declared her thoughts and intentions directly. She revived such old hits as "Fire Down Below," "Stay With Me, Baby," and "My Way," giving her unique interpretation to them. Also, the combination of song and wit as essential components of her performance linked Bette Midler to Mae West. Conveying a bold message with a smile on her face, she endeared herself to audiences, even if some thought she was shocking. Of course, audacity was highly prized among the young in the 1970s, and while West had to watch out for the censors, Midler had no such concerns.

In the 1980s and 1990s, Madonna surely qualified as an unconscious imitator of Mae West. Her sexy, outrageous, and audacious presentation of self in the concert halls was reminiscent of Mae West's spirit. Madonna spoofed sex as she danced her way across the stage. Whereas Mae West wore 1890s costumes to emphasize her sexual attractiveness, Madonna wore micromini skirts, halter tops, and underwear as outerwear. Madonna flaunted her sexual appeal, often to audiences of preadolescent girls. Her audience, of course, was a dramatically different one from both West's and Midler's. The common ingredient they all shared was an eagerness to test the conventional waters about sexuality, male-female relations, and public displays of private material. Mae West might have been surprised, even shocked, by some of Madonna's concert appearances, but she would have recognized the link to her style.

Mae West began as an outsider in popular entertainment and became an insider. Most entertainers who begin on the fringe remain on the fringe. Unless they have the capacity to alter their act, they cannot hope for an opportunity to perform on television. Despite the loosening of the censor's grip in recent years, curses, nudity, and off-color jokes cannot appear on network television—on pay cable channels, perhaps, but not on mainstream television. Today, outrageous performers can achieve great popularity in the movies or on the concert stage. Mae West did not have the same freedom, but she refused to change her style to accommodate the mainstream. She sought the big time, and she succeeded, never altering her Diamond Lil persona, never changing her one-liners, her swaggers, and her nasal delivery.

Mae West's body did not fit the stereotypical ideals of beauty for women early in the century. She was not the small, lithe, ingenue type, nor was she the burly burlesque comic woman. She fell somewhere in between and insisted on her uniqueness. She baldly declared that she was attractive and defied the existing formulas, creating her own. Her great self-confidence was probably the trait that both attracted and astonished her followers. West's brash self-assertiveness was unique; it broke everyone's expectations. She always dismissed imitators as poor shadows who never came close to the original. She was the sole source of her truth and power and no one could compete, compare, or equal her style. This attitude, which she maintained consistently throughout a sixty-odd-year career, became the central feature of her endurance. Her confidence never deserted her; neither did her sense of humor.

Where should Mae West be placed in American cultural history? What role did she play in the history of American women? As suggested throughout this book, her public life was played out on stages, in night clubs, and on movie sets. She was one of the most visible women of the twentieth century. She not only struck down the conventional boundaries between the private world of women and the public life of men, but she moved the private into the public domain. She spoke about forbidden subjects in public in a decidedly unladylike fashion and in public spaces that had formally been reserved for men only. It can never be known exactly how much space she occupied in the American imagination, but it is clear from her loyal and continuous audience that she delighted millions over a very long period of time. She offered vicarious pleasure to both men and women. Although she may not have directly caused drastic changes in their behavior, she may have secretly caused mental questionings about the woman's role in sexual matters.

Cultural historians can only speculate on how much attention Americans give to their popular cultural pursuits. Do they think about last night's TV shows? If so, how much? Do they discuss them with friends? Do they take comedy and melodrama seriously? Although it is hard to obtain definitive answers to these questions, it is possible to gauge something from the television ratings, the movie attendance figures, box-office receipts, record sales, and newsprint devoted to the stars and their shows. From personal experiences, we know that we discuss our leisure activities with our friends and families. We describe the plots of our favorite TV soap operas to friends who missed an episode; we debate basketball strategy; and we share the latest gossip about our favorite stars. Surely Mae West provided many people, over a very long time, with lots of material to discuss.

Humor is a very serious business, as most comics will affirm. The pursuit of comedy requires skill, thoughtfulness, and careful analysis. But the tragedy of great comics is that their audience does not take them seriously. Further, the performing comic is a highly perishable commodity. Mae West's humor can still be seen on film, but her many years in vaudeville and in night clubs can never be recaptured or reproduced. So the humor of performers that is not captured on film or videotape never achieves the status or the memory of the writer's or the painter's art. Because the humorist evokes a laugh rather than a serious response from her audience, she is not regarded as respectfully as the "serious" commentator. Yet the insights, the common sense, and the wit of West's approach to life still ring true and qualify as part of the homespun philosophy Americans appreciate. Mae West contributed to the dialogue on male-female relations in America and she added spice and ammunition to the debate on censorship. She also reminded her fans never to take themselves too seriously. These are all lessons as appropriate to the 1990s audience as they were to previous ones.

Finally, Mae West was the ultimate self-promoter and a great example of the American entrepreneurial spirit. She did it by herself and for herself. She was an American individualist in the best male tradition—but she was a woman. As a result, her ambitions, efforts, and successes were not interpreted in the same way as those of men. Although she never spoke out for women's rights, her life and her work implicitly offered women alternative visions of women's roles, possibilities, and hopes. She was not a social activist, an organizer, or a member of any women's group. The only group she belonged to was the Mae West Fan Club. Rather, she was an American pioneer; she created herself, became a rugged individualist, and permanently imprinted her image on the American imagination.

BIBLIOGRAPHICAL ESSAY

The historian who seeks information on show business performers finds the task difficult, especially if the performer is one whose work was considered bawdy and unconventional. First-hand accounts are selective and biased, and reminiscences are colored by age and memory. However, when the performer achieves the celebrity and fame of Mae West, there are sources to consult, however fragile. The primary archival source, which yields a great deal of material on her early career, is in the Billy Rose Theater Collection of the New York Public Library. Clipping files containing newspaper stories on her various Broadway plays offer the historian a great deal of information on the reaction to *Sex, The Drag, Pleasure Man,* and her other plays. Feature stories, including photographs from the period, are also in the files. West's whole career can be recaptured by reading the extensive file collection in New York.

Viewing Mae West's movies is also possible today. Both the Library of Congress in Washington, D.C., and the Motion Picture Association Collection in Beverly Hills, California, have prints of her movies. Many are available on videocassette as well, so they are easily accessible to anyone interested in her film work. The censorship issue can be studied from the files in the manuscript division of the Library of Congress. The show business magazines of the period, such as *Equity,* the Actor's Equity magazine, also yield important information. The National Police *Gazette,* which had an entertainment page, and *Variety,* the most comprehensive source on the entertainment industry, are available on microfilm in most large libraries.

Within the Billy Rose Theater Collection are clipping files for many of the other vaudevillians to whom I compared Mae West in this biography. I consulted the source material on Eva Tanguay and Millie De Leon and found the comparison of careers and the similarities of audience response to these bawdy women entertainers very enlightening. Information on night club singer Sophie Tucker was also obtained at the New York Public Library. By looking at the files of many of West's contemporaries in burlesque, vaudeville, and the Broadway stage, the researcher is able to place her life and career within a larger context.

Reviews of her theatrical productions are available from the *New York Times* and *Variety,* as well as the reference source *The New York Theatre Critics' Reviews,* which is issued annually and is available in most libraries. The West Clipping Files in the Rose Collection also contain reviews of her road productions. Other libraries that have more limited West collections are those of the University of Wisconsin—Madison and the University of Southern California. Both also have large photographic collections that span Mae West's long career.

Mae West's autobiography, *Goodness Had Nothing to Do with It* (Englewood Cliffs, New Jersey, 1959) introduces the reader to a tame version of the larger-than-life personality. Various memoirs of show business personalities who knew and worked with Mae West offer additional perspectives. Adolph Zukor's *The Public Is Never Wrong* (New York, 1953) is a good example of the genre. Bowling Green State University's Popular Culture Center has some movie magazines of the 1930s; particularly good examples of feature articles on the stars can be found in *Movie Mirror* and *Motion Pictures.* Although Mae West was never featured as often as Joan Crawford or Greta Garbo, there were occasional stories about her exploits.

The current interest in women has yielded a doctoral dissertation on Mae West. Marybeth Hamilton's " 'When I'm Bad, I'm Better': Mae West and American Popular Entertainment" (Ph.D. dissertation, Princeton University, 1990) focuses upon the censorship issue and West's career, particularly the Broadway years and the first two years of her Hollywood experience. Jon Tuska's *The Films of Mae West* (New Brunswick, 1973) provides a good overview of her early years and a detailed discussion of each film's plot, cast of characters, and reception. Joseph Weintraub's *The Wit and Wisdom of Mae West* (New York, 1967) collects the many one-liners made famous by West.

The only full-length biography of Mae West is George Eells and Stanley Musgrove's *Mae West: A Biography* (New York, 1982). Musgrove did public relations work for West, and the biography relies on many first-hand accounts given by Hollywood insiders; however, there are no footnotes or bibliography, thereby making it hard for the history student to determine the validity of the information. Charles W. Stein, editor, *American Vaudeville as Seen by Its Contemporaries* (New York, 1984), provides the reader with many first-hand accounts of the favorite theaters and entertainers of the period.

Among the secondary sources that I found useful in preparing this biography were: Jill Dolan, *The Feminist Spectator as Critic* (Ann Arbor, Mich., 1988); Lewis A. Erenberg, *Steppin' Out: New York Nightlife and the Transformation of American Culture,* 1890–1930 (Westport, Conn., 1981); Caroline Caffin, *Vaudeville* (New York, 1914); Albert F. McLean, Jr., *American Vaudeville as Ritual* (Lexington, Ky., 1965); Charles and Louise Samuels, *Once Upon a Stage: The Merry World of Vaudeville* (New York, 1974); John E. DiMeglio, *Vaudeville, U.S.A.* (Bowling Green, Oh., 1973); and Douglas Gilbert, *American Vaudeville: Its Life and Times* (New York, 1940).

Additional sources that provide background and interpretive information are Karen M. Stoddard, *Saints and Shrews: Women and Aging in American Popular Film* (Westport, Conn., 1983); Molly Haskell, *From Reverence to Rape: The Treatment of Women in Film*

(New York, 1974); Andrew Bergman, *We're In the Money: Depression America and Its Films* (New York, 1971); Irving Zeidman, *The American Burlesque Show* (New York, 1967); Gerald Bordman, *American Musical Comedy: From Adonis to Dreamgirls* (New York, 1982); and Lawrence W. Levine, *Highbrow/Lowbrow* (Cambridge, Mass., 1988). For an understanding of the Hollywood Production Code, see Olga J. Martin, *Hollywood's Movie Commandments: A Handbook for Motion Picture Writers and Reviewers* (New York, 1937).

INDEX

Addams, Jane, 128
Albee, E. F., 9, 18
Amateur nights, 10–11
Ameche, Don, 88
Anna Christie, 58
Anthony, Susan B., 128
"Any Kind of Man," 21
Arden, Eve, 61
Armstrong, Louis, 87
Asch, Sholem, 36
Atkinson, Brooks, 102–3

Babe Gordon, 52
Ball, Lucille, 61
Barrett, Rona, 126
Beavers, Louise, 68, 112
Beebe, Lucius, 105
Belle of the Nineties, 79–81
Benchley, Robert, 53
Benevolent Order of Santa Clauses, 87
Bergen, Edgar, 88
Bernhardt, Sarah, 132
Birth of a Nation, 74
Bogart, Humphrey, 61, 122
Bow, Clara, 60
Breen, Joseph I., 69–70, 81
Brennan, Jay, 44
Brice, Fanny, 10, 11, 13, 33, 57, 73
Broadway, 9, 33
Buchman, Frank, 93
Burlesque, 4

Cagney, James, 61
Camille, 84
Canby, Vincent, 125
Capitol Theater, 34
Captive, The, 41, 46–47
Catherine Was Great, 96–97, 98, 99–101, 102
"Cave Girl," 20
Cavett, Dick, 125
Censorship, 30, 36–37, 41–42, 52, 69–70, 80–81, 83–84, 90
Chandler, Charlotte, 135–36
Chaplin, Charlie, 59, 132
Chapman, John, 100–1
Chesterfield Supper Club Show, 105–6
Chez Paree, 108
China Seas, 84
Clarendon, Hal, 10
Clurman, Harold, 103, 104
Coconut Grove Playhouse, 118
Cohen, Emanuel, 85, 86, 87, 91
Collingwood, Charles, 115–16
Come On Up . . . Ring Twice, 101, 108
Como, Perry, 105–6
Constant Sinner, The, 52–54
Conway, Jack, 52
Copa City, 108
"Copulating Blues," 73
Corbett, James J., 27
Cosell, Howard, 126
Cotton Club, 32–33
Crabtee, Lotta, 11

Crawford, Joan, 61
Cugat, Xavier, 86
Curtis, Tony, 126

Dale, Margaret, 88
Dalton, Timothy, 126
Daly's Theater, 38, 40, 48
Davis, Bette, 61, 91, 123, 136
De Leon, Millie, 17, 29–30
Delta Kappa Alpha, 122
De Luise, Dom, 126
Dempsey, Dolly, 109, 126
Dempsey, Jack, 27
Devil Is a Woman, The, 84
Diamond Lil, 6, 23, 40, 48–53, 55, 65, 69, 84–85, 101, 102, 103–6
Dickens, Charles, 11
Dietrich, Marlene, 60, 61, 84, 87, 136
Dillingham, Charles, 35
Drag, The, 41, 44, 46, 47, 53, 136

Edgewater Beach Playhouse, 118
Ellington, Duke, 68, 80
Eltinge, Julian, 44, 45
Every Day's a Holiday, 87, 90–91
Extra-sensory perception, 93

Female impersonators, 44–46, 136
Fields, W. C., 33, 91–92, 122
"Frankie and Johnny," 18, 49, 50, 65, 73, 107
Friml, Rudolf, 21

Gable, Clark, 61
Garbo, Greta, 58, 60, 61, 84, 123, 132
Gardner, Hy, 109
General Federation of Women's Clubs, 86
Gilbert, Douglas, 75
God of Vengeance, The (Asch), 36
Going to Town, 82

Goodness Had Nothing to Do with It (Autobiography), 7, 16, 17, 28, 47, 48, 60, 77, 79, 101, 112–13
Gotham Theater, 10
Go West, Young Man, 86
Grable, Betty, 101
Grant, Cary, 68, 71, 76, 92, 124
Gray Panthers, 128
Gray, Thomas J., 44
Greenwood, Charlotte, 34
"Guy What Takes His Time, A," 72, 73

Hall, Gladys, 71–72
Hall, Mordaunt, 79
Hammerstein, Arthur, 21
Hargitay, Mickey, 110–11
Harlem, 32
Harlow, Jean, 61, 84
Hathaway, Henry, 85
Hayes, Helen, 97
Hays, Will, 69, 81
Hays Office, 81, 86
Hayworth, Rita, 101
Hearst, William Randolph, 81
Heat's On, The, 94–95
Hepburn, Katharine, 58, 91, 123
"He's a Bad, Bad Man, but He's Good for Me," 82
Hoffman, Gertrude, 30
Hogan, Willie, 15
Homosexuality, 46, 111–12, 137
Hope, Bob, 114, 125
Hopper, Hedda, 107–8
Horne, Harriet Van, 114
Howell, Chauncey, 124
Hudson, Rock, 114

"I Can't Give You Anything but Love," 114
"I'd Rather Be Blue Over You Than Happy With Someone Else," 73

"I Found a New Way to Go to Town," 76

"I Like To Do All Day What I Do All Night," 107

"I'm an Occidental Woman in an Oriental Mood," 83

"I May Add an Extra Fellow Here and There," 117

"I'm No Angel," 76

I'm No Angel, 68, 76, 78–79, 92

Irwin, May, 33

It Ain't No Sin, 79

Italian Village, 108

"It's So Nice to Have a Man Around the House," 117

"I Want You—I Need You," 76

"I Wonder Where My Easy Rider's Gone," 72, 73

Jazz music, 33

Jazz Singer, The, 58

Jennings, C. Robert, 131–32

Johnson, Lyndon B., 120

Johnson, Walter, 109

Jolson, Al, 13

Jones, Gorilla, 82

Joplin, Janis, 124

Kaufman, Al, 62–63

Keaton, Buster, 59

Keith, B. F., 9

Keith-Albee vaudeville circuit, 9, 14–15

Kelly, Thomas Jack, 93

Kingsbury, Rolly, 46

Klondike Annie, 82–84, 86, 92

Knight, Gene, 108

Krasner, Chuck, 110

Lasky, Jesse, 61

"Last a Long, Long Time," 107

Latin Quarter, 108

LeBaron, William, 62, 65–66

Levine, Lawrence, 3

Lewis, R. W. B., 127

Liberty magazine, 43

Little Nell the Marchioness, 11

Lloyd, Harold, 59

Loew's State Theater, 9, 23

Loews, The (Marcus Loew and son, Arthur M.), 9

Lombard, Carole, 61

Long, Barbara, 125, 127–28

Lopez, Vincent, 82

"Love is Love in any Woman's Heart," 82

Loy, Myrna, 61

Lubin, Arthur, 117

Lubitsch, Ernst, 61, 85–86

Mabley, Moms, 11, 20, 57

Madden, Owney, 25

Made in France, 107

Madonna, 1, 138

Mae West Fan Club, 141

"Mamma Goes Where Poppa Goes," 73

Mansfield, Jayne, 110–11

Martin, Dean, 114

Martin, Dean, Show, 118

Mast, Jane (pen name), 38

Mayer, Arthur, 74–75, 113

Mayo, Archie, 63

McCarey, Leo, 80, 85

McCarthy, Charlie, 88

McCourt, James, 136

Melodramas, 34

Merman, Richard, 132

Metro-Goldwyn-Mayer (MGM), 61, 66

Midler, Bette, 137–38

Model Theater, 17

Moral Rearmament movement, 93

Morganstern, Clarence, 42–43

Moseley, Leonard, 102

Motion Picture Producers and Directors Association, 69
"Moving' Day," 8
"Mr. Ed," 117, 118
Muir, Helen, 118
Murrow, Edward R., 115
My Little Chickadee, 91–92
"My Mariocch-Make-Da-Hoochy-Ma-Coocha in Coney Island," 8
Myra Breckinridge, premiere of, 6, 123–25

Nassour, Ellis, 134–35
Nathan, George Jean, 77
National Vaudeville Artists Association, 14
Newman, Lionel, 90
New Movie Magazine, 67
New York Anti-Vice Society, 36
Night After Night, 62–63
Night clubs, 32–33
Nixon, Richard, 121
Novak, Paul, 110, 111, 118, 124, 134
Nugent, Frank, 83, 92

O'Connor, John J., 125
Old Curiosity Shop (Dickens), 11
Opera, 3–4
Organized crime, 37

Palace Theater, 23
Paramount Studios, 61–64, 66, 68–69, 70, 74–75, 76, 78, 79, 85, 87, 91
Park Theater, 47
Passing Show of 1919, The, 33–34
Pastor, Tony, 4
Perelman, S. J., 83
Personal Appearance, 86
"Person to Person" show, 115–16
Phelan, Kappo, 99
Pickford, Mary, 10

Pleasure Man, 51–52, 54
Pollock, Arthur, 99
Powell, William, 61
Presley, Elvis, 135
Prohibition, 33

Raft, George, 62, 63
Red Skelton Show, 116–17
Reles, Kid Twist, 94
Rhodes, Robert, 94
Ribonsky, Chester, 110
Richman, Harry, 18, 21, 23
Ring, Blanche, 33
Roberts, Steven V., 122
Romano, Liboria, 99
Rossell, Deac, 124
Royale Theater, 48

Sahara Hotel, 108
Savoy, Bert, 44, 45
Scarlet Empress, The, 87
Sennwald, Andre, 80
Sex, 30, 38–41, 43, 53, 129–30
Sextette, 117–18, 125–26
She Done Him Wrong, 64, 65, 66, 68, 70–71, 72–76, 77–78, 79, 87, 92, 109, 117, 127
Sherman, Lowell, 73
Shubert Theater, 9, 35, 48
Shuberts, The, 9, 35
Siegel, Bugsy, 94
Silent films, 9
Silverman, Sime, 17–18, 20–21, 23, 29
Sisk, Bob, 39
Smith, Bessie, 4, 11, 20, 73
Sobel, Louis, 109
Sometime, 21
Southern California Council of Federal Church Women, 86
Stanwyck, Barbara, 91
Stein, Herb, 108–9
Sukul, Sri Deva Ram, 93

Sullivan, Ed, 78, 115
Sunday, Billy, 12

"Take It Easy, Boys," 107
Tanguay, Eva, 10, 11, 16–17, 19, 22, 23, 29, 30, 33, 57, 137
Taylor, Frank, 125
Taylor, Robert, 61, 84
Theatrical Owners Booking Association, 13–14
"They Call Me Sister Honky-Tonk," 76
Thomas, Bob, 133
Thompson, J. Walter, agency, 88
Timony, James, 37–38, 40, 42–43, 44, 47, 60, 62, 68, 78, 94, 101, 110
Todd, Michael, 96–97
Troy, William, 77
Tucker, Sophie, 16, 19, 22, 30, 57, 73, 137
Turner, Lana, 101
Twentieth Century Limited, 58

United Booking Office, 14–15

Van Horne, Harriet, 118
Vaudeville shows, 4, 8–9, 10, 33
    amateur nights in, 10–11
    black circuit in, 13–14
    change of acts in, 13
    customers in, 14
    demanding schedule in, 13
    family night in, 14
    pay scale of, 14
    popularity of, 14
Verrill, Addison, 124
Victorian age, impact of, on theater, 11–13
Vidal, Gore, 123
Virgin Man, The, 41, 42

Walker, Jimmy, 41, 42
Wallace, Frank, 15–16, 50, 94
    reappearance of, 94
Walsh, Raoul, 82–84, 85
Warner Brothers, 58
Wayburn, Ned, 34
Welch, Raquel, 123
West, Beverly (sister), 7, 11, 78, 112
West, John (brother), 7
West, John Patrick (father), 7
West, Mae
    abdominal problems of, 105
    ability of, 13
    accusation of, as female impersonator, 45–46
    act with sister, Beverly, 20–21
    ambition of, 28–29, 35, 38, 134
    appeal of, 59–60
    appearance at Delta Kappa Alpha awards banquet, 122
    appearance in *Made in France,* 107
    appearance in New Haven, 21
    appearance of, on Chase and Sanborn Hour, 88–90
    appearance of, on Dean Martin Show, 114–15
    appearance of, on "Mr. Ed," 117, 118
    appearance of, on Red Skelton Show, 116–17
    appearances on Chesterfield Supper Club Show, 105–6
    appearance with Rock Hudson, 114
    arrest of, 41–42
    arrival in Hollywood, 59–60
    association of, with Timony, 37–38, 40, 44, 47, 60, 68, 78, 94, 101
    at amateur nights, 10–11
    audience reaction to, 18, 19, 20, 21, 30, 35–36, 52, 53, 71–72, 73–77, 86, 106, 125

West, Mae, continued
  autobiography of, 7, 16, 17, 28, 47,
    48, 60, 77, 79, 101, 112–13
  bawdy style of, 19–20, 22, 35, 50,
    55, 73, 79, 98–99, 122, 129
  biracial theme of, 111–12
  birth of, 7
  and British naming of life jackets
    after, 95
  British tour of, 101–2
  Broadway years of, 15, 22–23,
    55–56
  Brooklyn accent of, 25, 58
  celebrity status of, 97–98
  and censorship, 30, 36–37, 41–42,
    52, 69–70, 80–81, 83–84, 90
  change of name from Mary Jane,
    7
  "character" songs of, 24
  as child star, 10–11
  and Cohen, 91
  and competition, 60
  as competitive, 23–24
  conviction of, 43
  critical reviews of performance,
    17–18, 20–21, 23, 25, 29–30,
    38–39, 48, 49–50, 52–53, 53, 73,
    75, 77, 78, 79, 80, 81, 84, 92,
    97–99, 100–1, 102–4, 105, 107–9,
    111–12, 114–15, 118, 124–25
  current affairs interests of, 120–22
  death of, 126
  and death of Timony, 110
  as Diamond Lil, 40, 75, 84–85
  divorce of, 94
  drawing power of, 91
  durability of, 104
  early childhood of, 7–8
  earnings of, 16–17, 81
  education of, 10, 133
  egocentricity of, 44, 131
  ego of, 59, 86–87, 105

  escorts of, 110
  facial features of, 34, 35
  family of, 7
  fan club membership, 109–10
  and film medium, 59–60
  films of, 66–69
  financing of plays of, 60
  flamboyance of, 64
  friendship with Owney Madden,
    25
  gags of, 18
  health concerns of, 104–5, 120, 127,
    133
  Hollywood recognition of, 122–23
  and homosexuality, 46, 111–12, 137
  humor of, 30, 66, 128, 140
  image of, 138–41
  individualism of, 132–33
  interest in shaping own material,
    38
  interest of, in boxing/wrestling,
    27, 82
  interest of, in Hollywood, 57–58
  interests in seances and
    spiritual life, 92–94
  invitation to Johnson White
    House, 120
  jail sentence of, 30, 43
  legal battles of, 47
  legendary status of, 1–2
  longevity of, 3, 6, 98
  male friends of, 28
  on marriage and family, 129–31
  marriage to Frank Wallace, 15–16,
    50
  merger of public and private
    personality, 23
  modern imitators of, 136–38
  morality trial of, 42–43
  nightclub appearances of, 21, 24,
    106–10, 118

West, Mae, continued

nonappearance of, on "Person to
Person," 115-16

one liners of, 59, 61, 65, 71, 72,
76-77, 82, 86, 90-91, 114, 119

at Paramount Studios, 61-64, 66,
68-69, 70, 74-75, 76, 78, 79, 85,
87, 91

under pen name of Jane Mast, 38

as perfectionist, 48

performance of, at Capitol
Theater, 34

performance of shimmy by, 17, 21, 22

personal appearances of, 64-65,
90, 97-98, 101, 104, 117-18

personal style of, 34

philosophy of life of, 79, 118-19,
120-21, 134-36

physical appearance of, 27, 98,
134, 139

at premiere of *Myra Breckinridge*, 6,
123-25

program notes for, 50

public image of, 55, 77-78, 101-2,
127-28

publicity for, 36, 75

public opinion of, 81-82

radio publicity campaign of, 87-90

reappearance of husband, Frank,
94

relations with directors, 85-86

relations with other women, 28

renegotiation of contract with
Paramount, 78-79

return to live theater, 117-18

and review of autobiography, 113

roles of, 54-55

in *Belle of the Nineties*, 79-81

in *Catherine Was Great*, 96-97, 98,
99-101, 102

in *Come On Up...Ring Twice*, 101,
108

in *Constant Sinner*, 52-54

in *Diamond Lil*, 6, 23, 40, 48-53,
55, 65, 69, 84-85, 101, 102, 103-6

in *The Drag*, 41, 44, 46, 47, 53, 136

in *Every Day's a Holiday*, 87, 90-91

in *Going to Town*, 82

in *Go West Young Man*, 86

in *Heat's On*, 94-95

in *I'm No Angel*, 68, 76, 78-79, 92

in *Klondike Annie*, 82-84, 86, 92

in *Little Nell the Marchioness*, 11

in *My Little Chickadee*, 91-92

in *Night After Night*, 62-63

in *Pleasure Man*, 51-52, 54

in *Sex*, 30, 38-41, 43, 53, 129-30

in *Sextette*, 117-18, 125-26

in *She Done Him Wrong*, 64, 65, 66,
68, 70-71, 72-76, 77-78, 79, 87,
92, 109, 117, 127

in *Sometime*, 21

in *Wicked Age*, 47-48

self-confidence of, 20, 120, 139

self-esteem of, 105, 118

on sex appeal, 72

as sex comedienne, 60-61

and sex-role reversal, 73, 75-76, 89

sexual image of, 2, 4-5, 18, 20,
27-28, 35, 38, 44, 86, 103,
111,127-28

sexual values of, 25-26

signing with Cohen as producer,
85

songs of, 72-73

"Any Kind of Man," 21

"Cave Girl," 20

"Frankie and Johnny," 18, 49,
50, 65, 73, 107

"Guy What Takes His Time,
A," 72, 73

"He's a Bad, Bad Man, but
He's Good for Me," 82

West, Mae, songs of, *continued*
"I Can't Give You Anything but
  Love," 114
"I Found a New Way to Go to
  Town," 76
"I Like To Do All Day What I
  Do All Night," 107
"I'm an Occidental Woman in an
  Oriental Mood," 83
"I May Add an Extra Fellow
  Here and There," 117
"I'm No Angel," 76
"It's So Nice to Have a Man
  Around the House," 117
"I Want You—I Need You," 76
"I Wonder Where My Easy
  Rider's Gone," 72, 73
"Last a Long, Long Time," 107
"Love is Love in any Woman's
  Heart," 82
"Moving' Day," 8
"My Mariocch-Make-Da-
  Hoochy-Ma-Coocha in Coney
  Island," 8
"Take It Easy, Boys," 107
"They Call Me Sister
  Honky-Tonk," 76
as song writer, 20
staircase line of, 71
stroke of, 126
studio acceptance of, 79, 85–86,
  87, 91
as subject of female
  impersonators, 136
success of, 24–25
as symbol of modern woman,
  75–76
television appearances of, 113–17

timing of career, 8
tour with Willie Hogan, 15
underworld theme in shows of, 41,
  53
unwillingness of, to share
  spotlight, 21
use of media by, 94
and value of timing as film
  technique, 63
values of, 123
on vaudeville circuit, 11–12, 14–15,
  18, 20, 35, 65
wisecracking by, 61
on women's sexuality, 131–32
work schedule of, 87
and World War II, 97
writing of article for *Liberty*
  magazine, 43
writings of, 44, 46
West, Mary Jane. *See* West, Mae
West, Matilda Doelger (mother),
  7, 19
Wicked Age, The, 47–48
Williams, Bert, 33
Winter, Johnny, 124
Wit and Wisdom of Mae West, 119
Wright, Chalky, 82, 111

Young, Stark, 98–99

Ziegfeld, Florenz, 9, 33, 35
Ziegfeld Follies, 9, 13, 33
Zukor, Adolph, 61, 63, 65–66, 71,
  74–75

Mae West: She Who Laughs, Lasts was copyedited by Anita Samen. Sponsoring editor was Maureen Hewitt. Production editor was Lucy Herz. Picture research was done by Gillian Speeth, Picture This. The text was typeset by Point West, Inc., and printed and bound by McNaughton & Gunn.

Book design by Roger Eggers.